ISAIAH

Living Word BIBLE STUDIES

ISAIAH

The Lord Saves

KATHLEEN BUSWELL NIELSON

P&R
PUBLISHING
P.O. BOX 817 • PHILLIPSBURG • NEW JERSEY 08865-0817

Printed in the United States of America

ISBN: 978-1-62995-589-6

CONTENTS

v

CONTENTS

FOREWORD

Books that share the name of a prophet are generally over-looked today by Bible readers. We have convinced ourselves that the vast difference in time and custom between their world and our own presents a chasm too great for us to cross. In addition, their literary dependence on formal discourse is at odds with our preferred style of casual conversation. Further, knowing how these ancient works should be applied to contemporary readers appears to require an art form beyond our own set of skills. And if these reasons are not enough, the sheer length of a book like Isaiah can often deter us. Yes, truth be told, we often pass over the prophetic books, especially one like Isaiah, in favor of others we consider to be more accessible, easy to finish, and ready to apply.

Yet we should know that our persistent neglect of Isaiah can't be a good thing. After all, this prophetic book had an enormous role in establishing God's "good news" in the world. Isaiah is quoted in the New Testament more than any other book in the Old Testament. Mark chose to open and explain his gospel with it. The whole of Paul's literary corpus made extensive use of it. Philip was able to lead a man to Christ by it. And Jesus went so far as to ground his entire ministry in it (Luke 4:16–21).

Given Isaiah's place of prominence in the gospel, perhaps it is time for us to commit to the work of reading and understanding it well. After all, according to the apostolic gospel, a careful reading of Isaiah refreshes the one who truly desires a heart that is warm toward God. For here, we see the heart of God expressed in the fullness of his just judgments and mercy. Isaiah lived during the days of Judah's lesser savior-kings—and he served God by proclaiming to them (and to us) that God's greater One was yet to come. Through Isaiah's prophecy, God's people were given a just sentence for their failings, comfort for their sins, and a reason for their hope. In short, Isaiah presents us with a God who keeps all his promises—including the good news of rebuilding a people for relationship with him by sending us his promised Son. Who can read this work and not sit in rapt attention to the songs that only God's Suffering Servant could rightly sing? But who can read this book and not end up singing a new song of praise to God for the salvation he brings through the coming of his King?

In preparing these studies on the prophet Isaiah, Kathleen Nielson has done all of us a huge favor. By that I mean she has already done much of the heavy lifting. In doing so, she has cleared the way for us to come to a better understanding of this part of God's Word. Her commentary guides us across terrain we first thought impassible. Her writing style both piques and retains our interest along the way. And her routine attention to questions of application will bring the message of the book home to our hearts on a regular basis. If you are someone who has not yet read and studied Isaiah over a definite period of time, I can only say that at some level I envy you—for there is nothing quite like coming across treasures of this magnitude for the first time!

David R. Helm

A PERSONAL WORD
FROM KATHLEEN

I began to write these Bible studies for the women in my own church group at College Church in Wheaton, Illinois. Under the leadership of Kent and Barbara Hughes, the church and that Bible study aimed to proclaim without fail the good news of the Word of God. What a joy, in that study and in many since, to see lives changed by the work of the Word, by the Spirit, for the glory of Christ.

In our Bible study group, we were looking for curriculum that would lead us into the meat of the Word and teach us how to take it in, whole Bible books at a time—the way they are given to us in Scripture. Finally, one of our leaders said, "Kathleen—how about if you just write it!" And so began one of the most joyful projects of my life: the writing of studies intended to help unleash the Word of God in people's lives. The writing began during a busy stage of my life—with three lively young boys and always a couple of college English courses to teach—but through that stage and every busy one since, a serious attention to studying the Bible has helped keep me focused, growing, and alive in the deepest ways. The Word of God will do that. If there's life and power in these studies, it is simply the life and power of the Scriptures to which they point. It is ultimately the life and power of the Savior who shines through all the Scriptures from beginning to end. How we need this life, in the midst of every busy and non-busy stage of our lives!

I don't think it is just the English teacher in me that leads me to this conclusion about our basic problem in Bible study these days: we've forgotten how to *read*! We're so used to fast food that we think we should be able to drive by the Scriptures periodically and pick up some easily digestible truths that someone else has wrapped up neatly for us. We've disowned that process of careful reading, observing the words, seeing the shape of a book and a passage, asking questions that take us into the text rather than away from it, and digging into the Word and letting it speak! Through such a process, guided by the Spirit, the Word of God truly feeds our souls. Here's my prayer: that, by means of these studies, people would be further enabled to read the Scriptures profitably and thereby find life and nourishment in them, as we are each meant to do.

In all the busy stages of life and writing, I have been continually surrounded by pastors, teachers, and family who encourage and help me in this work, and for that I am grateful. The most wonderful guidance and encouragement come from my husband, Niel, whom I thank and for whom I thank God daily.

May God use these studies to lift up Christ and his Word, for his glory!

INTRODUCTION

What a treasure we have in the book of Isaiah: God's inspired word through his prophet; some of the most beautiful poetry in the Bible; a theological masterpiece (sometimes called the "Romans of the Old Testament"); a glimpse into God's perspective on human history; a magnificent presentation of his redemptive plan. Isaiah is a large book, not just in number of words and chapters. The prophet's "vision" (Isa. 1:1) given to him as the very word of the Lord (Isa. 1:2) involves insight into truths that stretch from creation to the final day, from Mount Zion in Jerusalem to the Zion that will someday encompass the whole re-created earth. Isaiah was enabled by God to see and to communicate what the course of history looks like to the one who ordains all of it. It is a dizzying prospect.

The goal in writing this study has not been to simplify this complex book, but to encourage and enable people to read it with growing understanding and joy. Often we hear the better-known passages from Isaiah (especially at Christmas and Easter), and we sense that they form part of a great, huge work, but we lack a grasp of the whole book and just how these wonderful passages fit in. That grasp is truly accessible with some hard work and steady, prayerful reading—and with the aid of the Holy Spirit who promises to help us understand. We will not end by having mastered all the deep intricacies and treasures of Isaiah; the goal here is to end by having understood the shape and themes of the book, by having read it through and examined it with loving care, and by having prepared ourselves for further, lifelong study and delight in this book. In order to create just 24 lessons, it has been necessary to bite off some large chunks—all of which would bear more detailed study. However, the benefit of pushing through the whole book is that we indeed gain a sense of the whole and of how beautifully the parts hold together. Even as we push through, though, there cannot help but be many moments of pausing to marvel over individual verses and passages. Isaiah will stop us often, taking our breath away with the beauty of his vision and the personal voice of God speaking to us, his people.

Reading this book with understanding and joy will necessarily involve connecting with it personally. However, this will not always mean that we will go away from a lesson with a list of things we can do to apply the text. Sometimes this may mean we are changed by understanding more about God's marvelous plan of redemption of which we are a part. The most fundamental revelation of Isaiah is a revelation of God and how he works his redemptive plan through all of history: that is why Day Five of each lesson asks first a question focusing on what we have seen about God in the text. Of course, then, our role is to take this revelation into our hearts, apply it in our prayers—*and*, yes, live according to it. That was the problem with God's people in Isaiah's time: they did not believe and so *live* according to the truth they had been given about God in his Law and through his prophets.

To apply this book, we should first apply it to ourselves as the people of God. The line of connection from the Jews of Jerusalem does not move to America or any other nation; it does not move first even to individual believers; it moves first to the church, the body of Christ. As the apostle Paul puts it, "It is those of faith who are the sons of Abraham. And the Scripture, foreseeing that God would justify the Gentiles by faith, preached the gospel beforehand to Abraham, saying, 'In you shall all the nations be blessed'" (Gal. 3:7–8). Isaiah preaches this very message, pointing repeatedly to a faithful remnant of the Jews who will someday grow into God's gathered people from all the nations. Being Jewish didn't do it: Israel and even Judah, as we shall see, get piled right in there with all the other nations judged for their sin. But trust in the Lord for salvation and resulting heartfelt obedience to his law *did* do it—for the believing remnant and for all those of faith who would come after, including us. Isaiah lets us see ourselves as part of a called-out people of faith from all the nations of the world. It also spurs us on to spread that faith to all the nations, until the day when Jesus comes again.

The seed of Abraham points not only to the body of believers God will gather in; the seed points most fundamentally to the promised one who came from Abraham's seed to accomplish this salvation for God's people, who clearly cannot do it for themselves. Abraham's seed grew into a great nation that eventually established itself as a kingdom in the land God promised. God's promises unfolded to reveal a coming king from that seed and specifically from the tribe of Judah and the line of David—a king who would reign forever. As the Jewish kings came and went, and as the kingdom split into two parts which both declined and eventually were conquered, God's faithful people held on to his promise. Isaiah showed them how to do that by revealing the Promised One as a divine *king*, as a *servant*, and then as a *conqueror* who would finally come and rule over all the world. In pointing to Jesus Christ, the promised Messiah in the line of David, Isaiah gives hope to God's people in a time of darkness and collapse.

By the inspiration of the Holy Spirit, Isaiah was enabled to point to the Messiah. With the help of the Holy Spirit may we see Jesus our Savior in this book, either more clearly or perhaps for the first time. Not only in the New Testament but also in the Old, and particularly in Isaiah, Jesus Christ shines out as the one in whom God provides forgiveness of sins and saving hope. Salvation means being delivered not only *into* fellowship with God and God's people but also *from* his judgment. God's title repeated throughout Isaiah is "the Holy One of Israel." A holy and just God must judge sin, and Isaiah makes God's judgment vivid, both throughout history and on that last day to which Isaiah often refers—a day not only of final salvation but also of final judgment. In this context of God's holy wrath, we see redemption shining out all the more brilliantly in Isaiah. Isaiah's name in the Hebrew means "The LORD saves"; that is what this book is all about. That is what the Bible is all about. With good reason, Isaiah is quoted in the New Testament more than all the other prophets combined. We shall see examples and learn from the way the New Testament interprets the Old—always pointing to Jesus.

Lesson One will provide more specific introduction to the book. One comment about the much-debated issue of authorship: the first lesson treats this issue and exposes the controversies, but it does so from the perspective of one committed to the prophet Isaiah as single author of a unified book. Further discussion can be found in the works listed in the Notes—especially in Alec Motyer's *Isaiah*, which has been a hugely helpful background source for the writing of the study. Motyer's discussion of Isaiah's authorship is extremely clear and well presented, in both his introduction and his appendix.[1] All the listed bibliographical sources can be helpful, but I encourage first and foremost a careful reading of the text of Isaiah itself. Included in the course of the lessons are many notes (more than in my other studies) concerning background and context, which should provide enough information to read the text with basic understanding—and that is the goal.

Do spend your study time focusing on the Word, passage by passage, as this study leads you to do. Some of the questions may seem easier or harder; they reflect the complexity of this beautiful, many layered book. That said, I encourage you to use the questions flexibly. If one seems difficult, don't let it halt you; keep moving! There may be some questions, or parts of some, that you might want to wait on or come back to. The point is to spend the great majority of time taking in and musing on the Scripture itself. The Bible's living and active words are the words that change our hearts and lives, by the power of the Spirit.

May God, through his Spirit, open our ears and our eyes to the Word of the Lord through his prophet Isaiah.

1. Alec Motyer, *Isaiah: An Introduction and Commentary* (Downers Grove, IL: InterVarsity Press, 1999), 27–35, 297–301.

Lesson 1

THE LORD HAS SPOKEN

What a huge and happy prospect: to read this monumental book from beginning to end. This introductory lesson will help prepare us to read Isaiah with its contexts clear: the prophetic context, the historical context, and the literary context.

DAY ONE—THE PROPHETIC CONTEXT

1. The opening verse might serve as a heading for the whole book, as the prophet introduces this "vision"—a word that denotes a special revelation from God. First, read Isaiah 1:1–2b (i.e., through the second line of v. 2), and write down several specific observations about how the prophet Isaiah presents his book. (See also Isa. 2:1, introducing an initial section of the book.)

2. In the Bible, a prophet is one who communicates the words of God. What similarities do you notice in comparing the opening verses of Jeremiah (1:1–2), Amos (1:1–3), and Micah (1:1–2) with those of Isaiah?

3. How do the prophets fit in to the Bible's story? Early on, there were *non-writing prophets*, who spoke God's word but did not compile their prophecies in books. As you read the following verses, write down observations about some of these early prophets.

    a. Exodus 34:29–33; Deuteronomy 34:10–12

b. I Samuel 3:19–21

c. I Kings 21:17–19

4. Moving through the Old Testament in English, we find
the *writing prophets* beginning with Isaiah and ending with
Malachi. These prophets are classified as "major" and
"minor" simply depending on the length of their writ-
ings. (Isaiah is major!) They spoke into a dark part of
the story. God had promised to bless the descendants of
Abraham and all the nations of the earth through them.
Yet, after God redeemed them from slavery in Egypt,
gave them the law to show them how to live, and settled
them in the land he had promised them—even after
all that, they turned away from God. As they became
great, they disobeyed God and suffered disastrous con-
sequences. The prophetic books generally address at
least four central themes: the people's *disobedience*, the
resulting punishment and exile from their land, a *call to heed*

God's Word, and God's gracious *promises to restore them*. Look briefly through Isaiah 1:18–26. What phrases evidence these four themes?

5. The writing prophets pointed not only to the relatively near future of exile and restoration but also to the distant future: to the heavenly prophet who would come and perfectly fulfill all God's promises to his people. Comment briefly, as you read the following verses, on how the New Testament brings the climax toward which all the Old Testament prophets were pointing?

   a. Mark 1:1–9

b.   Hebrews 1:1–2

DAY TWO—THE HISTORICAL CONTEXT

1. Look through the General Timeline and the Detailed Timeline on pages 358–59. What general observations would you make about the historical period during which Isaiah prophesied?

2. Examine also the map of Isaiah's world, which generally suggests the territory of the Assyrian Empire (700s B.C.) and then the Babylonian Empire (later

600s–500s B.C.). What do you notice? What strikes you, in relation to the world today?

Although his message applied to all God's people (and all nations of the world), Isaiah spoke mainly to Judah, the southern kingdom composed of the tribes of Judah and Benjamin, with Jerusalem as the capital city. Early in the growth of God's people under kings in this promised land, the northern ten tribes separated themselves and made Samaria their capital. (The northern kingdom was called Israel, although "Israel" could still refer to all God's people.) The southern kingdom of Judah, which stayed faithful to the kingly line of David, in general disobeyed God less thoroughly and consistently. Judah's captivity and exile at the hands of the Babylonians (which Isaiah foresaw) came much later than Israel's captivity and exile at the hands of the Assyrians. It was the exiles from Judah who were allowed finally to return to their land after the exile—as Isaiah also foresaw.

3. In Isaiah 1:1, find the four kings of Judah under whose reigns Isaiah lived. As you look through the following background chapters from the historical books,

what general observations would you make about each king?

a. Uzziah (2 Chron. 26)

b. Jotham (2 Chron. 27)

c. Ahaz (2 Chron. 28)

d. Hezekiah (2 Chron. 29)

DAY THREE—LITERARY CONTEXT, PART I: THE BOOK'S SHAPE AND THEME

1. It is crucial at the start to grasp the shape of the entire book, so that each section will find its place within the whole. Read Isaiah 1:21–23, and then 66:10–14. What transformation do you see in this book, which has sometimes been called a "tale of two cities"?

Judah's center was Jerusalem, and the center of Jerusalem was the temple on Mount Zion. This was the place where God showed his presence with his people and where they came to worship and offer sacrifices. Isaiah uses Jerusalem, as we shall see, to mean not only the physical city but also the spiritual reality to which that city points: the New Jerusalem, the people of God gathered in his presence forever. The overarching shape of Isaiah's prophecy might be expressed as the *transformation of Jerusalem from disobedience and destruction to eternal life and communion with God*.

2. But there's more. This transformation will be accomplished through a particular figure, one who in Isaiah's

first section rules as the perfect *king*, in contrast with the imperfect kings on every side.[1]

a. After the Preface in chapters 1–5 comes the opening call to Isaiah in chapter 6. What do you notice about the king in Isaiah 6:1?

b. The book's first main section (chapters 7–39) is framed by two "bookend" stories of kings under attack. What similarities do you notice in Isaiah 7:1–8 and 36:1–2?

3. First, then, chapters 1–39 focus on the *king*, through prophecies based in the Assyrian-dominated period leading to the northern kingdom's fall and exile. The second large section (chapters 40–55) focuses on a *servant* figure, looking ahead to the suffering of Judah during its exile under the

1. The book's main sections are generally acknowledged. However, I want to mention that my thinking about these sections has been greatly influenced by Alec Motyer's especially clear and helpful *Isaiah: An Introduction and Commentary* (Downers Grove, IL: InterVarsity Press, 1999).

Babylonians. These chapters also foresee the suffering of the Servant who will come to redeem this suffering people. Read and comment briefly on Isaiah 42:1–4.

4. Finally, in chapters 56–66, which foresee the return from exile (and a restoration that stretches far into the future), Isaiah envisions a *conqueror* who will restore God's people. Read and comment briefly on Isaiah 61:1–7.

Many modern commentators have noted these sections and claimed the existence of two or three different writers of this book. After all, how could one man living when Isaiah lived foresee all the events prophesied in these chapters? The key word is "prophesied," which implies a message given by God, who knows all of history before it happens. The words God gave Isaiah form a unified book, one that reveals a God who not only knows but indeed sovereignly determines all of human history—for his glorious saving purposes in the one who is the King, the Servant of the Lord, and the eternal Conqueror. *Through this one the Lord will save his people forever in that New Jerusalem.* This is the overarching and consistent theme of Isaiah's prophecy.

For a summary review of Isaiah's shape, please consult the outline on pages 355–56.

Day Four—Literary Context, Part II: The Book's Style

Isaiah is celebrated as a literary masterpiece not only because of its beautifully unified shape but also because of its masterful use of language. Critics have discerned a difference in style between the first section (chapters 1–39) and the others: the first section communicates in more of a preaching style, with perhaps less-exalted poetry than the rest of the book. It does not necessarily follow, however, that different writers were at work. Isaiah, at different times in his life, had varying and probably increasing amounts of time, experience, and understanding from which to draw in his inspired writing. His growing poetic depth only enhances the book's consistent thematic focus.

1. Isaiah combines varying writing styles throughout. What differences do you note in style and subject between chapters 35 and 36?

The whole book of Isaiah combines *poetry* (as in chapter 35) with *prose* (as in chapter 36). Some of the prose tells a story in narrative form, as in chapter 36, and some is closer to poetry (see chapter 4).

We should notice the poetry! Hebrew poetry is character-ized by units of parallel meaning, which we see in lines balanced against each other—usually with the second (and sometimes a third) line indented. Three kinds of *parallelism* are generally acknowledged:

- Sometimes the second line continues the meaning of the first (*synthetic* parallelism).

- Sometimes the second line contrasts with the meaning of the first (*antithetic* parallelism).

- Sometimes the second line repeats in some way the meaning of the first (*synonymous* parallelism).

2. In Isaiah 1:3, for example, we find two sets of synonymous parallelism. How does each second line deepen while basically repeating the thought of the first?

3. Besides parallelism, another central characteristic of Hebrew poetry—and most poetry—is the use of imagery (picture language). Taking time to notice and muse on the imagery is a crucial part of understanding especially the poetic parts of God's Word. Consider the pictures in verse 3 and verse 18 of chapter 1, for example. What

do these different pictures make you see, and what do they communicate?

4. The poem in Isaiah 5:1–7 develops one central image. What is that image, and what does it make you see and understand?

5. Why do you think God gave us so much of his Word in poetic form?

DAY FIVE—JUMPING IN

1. This lesson has aimed to provide context for the book of Isaiah. The book's preface in chapters 1–5 provides its own introductory context, setting the tone and themes for all that follows. On this final day, simply read through this preface, not stopping to figure everything out as you go. We will study it more in depth. But in this read-through, be on the lookout for themes that emerge repeatedly— themes this lesson has introduced and themes that will shape the entire book. Look for the initial unfolding of the main theme: that *God will save his people forever in the New Jerusalem, through his promised King/Servant/Conqueror.* Be praying, as you read, for eyes to see the Lord God who reveals himself through the words of this book.

2. In light of what we have seen so far, what would you pray as you begin to study this book? Write a prayer, asking God for his own guidance as you study, and thanking him for the gift of his revelation to us in Isaiah.

Notes for Lesson 1

Lesson 2 (Isaiah 1)

THE LORD CALLS THE COURT TO ORDER

Just as chapters 1–5 offer a preface to the whole book, so chapter 1 itself beautifully lays out the central themes to come: sinful disobedience, God's just punishment, his call to listen, and his promised restoration. We have seen the opening verse, which introduces the prophet, his message, and his historical context. Not much is known about Isaiah the man or his father Amoz. We shall see that Isaiah was married and had children. His open access to kings and priests might well indicate a prominent Judean family. One other fact is foundational as we enter this book, and it recalls the main theme: Isaiah's name means "The Lord saves."

DAY ONE—THE LORD LAYS OUT THE CHARGES (ISAIAH 1:1–8)

1. Isaiah's opening appeal calls the whole universe to attention! Many have noted that God's first words ring out like charges in a universe-wide courtroom. In Isaiah 1:2–3, in

what ways does the Lord's initial statement reveal both love and judgment?

2. In the lament (an expression of grief) of Isaiah 1:4, the heart of the problem is revealed. In the three groupings of parallel lines, how does each second (and that third) line move on to reveal an even deeper level of Israel's sinfulness?

3. The designation "Holy One of Israel" (v. 4) occurs repeatedly throughout Isaiah, pulling together all parts of the book with this consistent view of God—whose holiness implies not only moral perfection but also uniqueness, separateness, otherness. List all the names for God you

find in this first chapter. Comment briefly on each, and on their cumulative effect here at the start.

4. Sin against such a Holy One has disastrous results. How does the picture in Isaiah 1:5–6 vividly communicate these results? What details stand out to you, and why?

5. Even the land shows (and will show even more vividly) the effects of the people's sin. Consult the notes given, and then comment on Isaiah 1:7–8. What do these verses make you see and feel, as you read them line by line?

   Notes:
   - *The phrase "daughter of Zion" <u>personifies</u> the nation of God's people, picturing them all as one person, as do vv. 5–6. Zion*

refers most often to Jerusalem (cf. Lesson One, Day Three), so "Zion's daughter" would picture those who have been raised and nurtured as God's people in this place.

- *At harvest time, workers in the fields and vineyards would construct and live in booths or temporary huts, which were abandoned to decay after the harvest.*

DAY TWO—THE LORD CONVICTS BUT MAKES AN OFFER (ISAIAH 1:9–20)

1. Read the background on the cities of Sodom and Gomorrah in Genesis 18:16–21 and 19:23–29. Then read Isaiah 1:9–10 and comment on how these two verses evidence both judgment and mercy.

2. Isaiah 1:11–15 again lets us hear God's voice directly, as he unfolds his charges against his people. *Note: The practices mentioned had been commanded by God in the Mosaic law, in order to show his redeemed people how they were to worship him. "New moons," for example, were the sacrifices commanded at each month's beginning.*

    a. Write down all the words and phrases that show God's attitude toward these practices at this point in Israel's history.

    b. What words and phrases help explain why God would hate practices that he had commanded? To what is God responding here?

3. List the specific commands in Isaiah 1:16–17 that reveal what the Holy One of Israel requires of those who would come into his presence. Then consider how you might group these commands, what sort of heading you might give to each group, and why they are in this order. Write down any other responses or observations you have concerning these commands. *Note: the fatherless and the widow would have been among the most helpless in society, lacking the protection of a man.*

4. Our response might well include a sense of inadequacy to obey all these commands. Consider how Isaiah 1:18–20 brings comforting closure to this section—as well as leaving some unanswered questions. Spend some time musing on these verses.

   a. How does the Lord (who made us and knows us) appeal here to all parts of our being: mind, heart, imagination, etc.?

b. Contrast the two alternative paths and the results promised.

c. How does the final line of v. 20 rightly conclude this section? What other verses in this chapter does this verse echo?

Day Three—It's the Story of a City (Isaiah 1:21–26)

1. What progression do you see in relation to this city in Isaiah 1:21–26? What words stand out to you?

2. The chapter's tone continues with another lament, the first part of which (vv. 21–23) describes further the sin of Jerusalem—that is, of God's people. The first picture here is not unique to Isaiah. Read Jeremiah 2:20 and Hosea 1:2, as well as Isaiah 1:21. Comment on this picture and the various aspects of what it communicates.

3. Observe the sins described in Isaiah 1:21–23. Is there a common thread or two? Consider, too, how these evils specifically negate the commands in Isaiah 1:16–17.

4. This is the low point, at which the names and the mighty person of the Lord God enter, bringing the only possible solution to the problem. Muse on Isaiah 1:24–26.

   a. In Isaiah 1:24–25, as God addresses his people, what is shocking in his words? What is full of hope? *Note: "smelt away your dross" refers to a process of exposing gold or silver to fire in order to burn away impurities. What verse does this recall?*

   b. In Isaiah 1:26, what does this third "I will" aim to accomplish?

   c. Day Five of this lesson will get to this question, but let's begin to ask it here: in Isaiah 1:24–26, what can we learn about God?

DAY FOUR—HOW WILL THE CITY
BE RESTORED? (ISAIAH 1:27–31)

1. Isaiah 1:27 is a key verse. The word "redeemed" sums up the restoration promised throughout this chapter. Rescue from sin is promised here! Make as many observations as you can, from this verse and from the context of the three verses preceding it, about *who* will be redeemed and *how* that redemption will be accomplished.

2. As we see the biblical theme of redemption unfolded more fully throughout Isaiah, so also we will see unfolded the accompanying theme of final judgment for those who do not repent. In Isaiah 1:28–31, how do the words and images vividly communicate the dreadfulness of God's

judgment? *Note: The oaks and gardens of v. 29 refer to the pagan nature worship and fertility cults embraced by the Israelites.*

3. Isaiah was pointing most immediately to the coming judgment of the exile, which God's disobedient people would suffer before a remnant of them would be restored to the Promised Land. But we know that Isaiah was pointing also to an even greater redemption, through the Promised One in whom God's perfect justice and righteousness would meet. How can we who hold the complete Scriptures not stop here to marvel at the unfolding of this revelation in which Isaiah so beautifully participated? Read Ephesians 1:3–10 and Titus 2:11–14; 3:3–7. What themes do you find that are similar to those in Isaiah 1, and how do you see them completed in the person of Jesus Christ?

4. Lest we focus only partly on the New Testament's completion of the redemption theme, let us remember that throughout the Scriptures, God is revealing redemption *from judgment*—salvation from the just punishment for sin against the Holy One of Israel. Read, for example, 2 Thessalonians 1:5–10. What words and truths strike you?

DAY FIVE—CONCLUSIONS

Each final day of study will include similar questions, so that you can stand back and process the section we have studied.

1. Look back through this huge introductory chapter of Isaiah, focusing on the person of God: what we learn of him, his attributes, and his ways of dealing with human beings. Write down several aspects of God that stand out to you, and then write a personal response—which could be in the form of a prayer, or questions, or simply a few sentences responding to

the Lord God who speaks to us through the inspired words of this prophet who lived so long ago.

2. Look once more through the chapter and choose a verse or a short passage to write out and meditate on or commit to memory. Be ready to share with your group the ways in which you find this verse (or verses) challenging, helpful, beautiful, etc.

Notes for Lesson 2

Lesson 3 (Isaiah 2–5)

THE LORD DECREES BOTH JUDGMENT AND PEACE

After the grand thematic introduction of chapter 1, the book's large preface (chapters 1–5) continues with Isaiah's vision of the Lord's salvation and the Lord's judgment. This is a "meaty" lesson, but it will be worth the effort to grasp the flow of the preface. Keep on reading! Chapters 2–4 begin and end with pictures of hope which encase or "bookend" words of judgment. Finally, chapter 5 offers a sad song and a woeful message, leaving deep darkness into which the vision and call of chapter 6 will break.

DAY ONE—THE LAYERS OF DAYS TO COME (ISAIAH 2)

1. Isaiah 2 opens with another heading, perhaps used to introduce a subsection of the book. Whereas Isaiah 1 introduced the days of Judah's kings, Isaiah 2:2 speaks of the "latter days"—a term that reaches farther, most often in Scripture to the time initiated by Jesus' first coming

31

to earth and climaxed by his second coming to judge and to reign forever. Read Joel 2:28–32 with Acts 2:14–21; Hebrews 1:2; and 1 Peter 1:20. Write down words, phrases, and thoughts that strike you about these last or "latter" days in which we now live and which are not yet ended.

2. Read the magnificent poem in Isaiah 2:2–4 (also found in Micah 4:1–3; one writer evidently borrowed from the other). As you read this poem, which is rather like a picture with motion and sound, what do you see and understand? What is the nature of the hope here portrayed? *Note: "The mountain of the house of the Lord" turns our thoughts to Jerusalem's Mount Zion, the site of the temple to which the Israelites streamed regularly for worship and sacrifice. That temple mount, in that city, came to represent the presence of the one true Lord God with his people.*

3. Consider the ways in which this poem reaches ahead. How might we see this poem coming to life today? What parts of it do we still hope and long for?

4. In light of such a hope, how is the exhortation in Isaiah 2:5 appropriate, for God's people then . . . for God's people now . . . for *you*?

5. Against the background of that shining hope, Isaiah sets his dark contemporary reality. Analyze the list of wrongs he lays out in Isaiah 2:6–9. What is Isaiah's perspective on these wrongs?

6. Isaiah (along with many of the prophets) looked forward not only to immediate judgment but to an appointed "day" at the end of the latter days, a time of final salvation and final judgment. Read Isaiah 2:10–21, looking for its various descriptions of who will rise and what will be brought low (and why) in that day. Write down your specific observations.

7. In light of this coming day, how is the concluding exhortation in verse 22 appropriate, for God's people then . . . for God's people now . . . for *you*?

Day Two—Judgment throughout Society (Isaiah 3)

1. Focusing in on Judah and Jerusalem in chapter 3, Isaiah declares dreadful imminent judgment by "the Lord God of hosts." What is the nature of that judgment, in Isaiah 3:1–3, and what is the nature of the results of that judgment, in Isaiah 3:4–7?

2. After zooming in to the sad little domestic scene between two brothers (Isa. 3:6–7), the camera pulls back and lets the narrator offer a clear assessment.

   a. How does each second line of the two pairs in Isaiah 3:8 provide even deeper insight about the situation?

   b. How does verse 9 provide even deeper insight for the last line of verse 8?

   c. How does Isaiah 3:10–11 provide an important balance at this point?

3. In Isaiah 3:12–15, the Lord steps up to speak, taking his place to contend as if in a courtroom. What repeated words and key words indicate the substance of his argument?

4. A vivid final section of indictment targets the women. In Isaiah 3:16, 18–23, what do we learn of these "daughters of Zion"? How would you characterize them?

5. Many commentators see Judah's fall and exile foretold here—especially as the verbs change from plural to singular, and the focus switches from many women in Jerusalem to Jerusalem itself pictured again as a woman. What aspects of the description make this judgment vivid and real to us, in Isaiah 3:17–4:1?

DAY THREE—A SECOND POEM AND A PARABLE (ISAIAH 4:2–5:7)

1. We are learning already Isaiah's rhythm of contrasts. How does Isaiah 4:2 echo Isaiah 3:18 and 4:1—yet offer a dramatic contrast?

2. The picture of this "branch" grows in meaning throughout Isaiah and throughout Scripture. Briefly, with what sorts of things is the branch associated in the following verses?

   a. Isaiah 4:2

   b. Isaiah 11:1–10

   c. Jeremiah 23:5–6

   d. Zechariah 3:8–10

3. What is the particular focus of the promise of Isaiah
4:3–4? What previous verses do these verses bring to
mind? *Consider: in longing for Christ and his return, do we long
not just for happiness and an end to trouble but also for holiness and
an end to sin?*

4. Like the one in Isaiah 2:1–5, this picture turns our
gaze toward Mount Zion. First, read Exodus 13:21–22;
19:18, and then read Isaiah 4:5–6. What happens to the
picture? What does this "canopy" lead you to see and
understand?

5. The picture of branches and fruit leads us into the song of the vineyard, which begins chapter 5. (Where already in Isaiah have we seen vineyards used to talk about God's people?) Read all but the last two lines of Isaiah 5:1–2. What details stand out as Isaiah sings this parable-like love song about his beloved Lord's care for his people?

6. Of course you read the last two lines! What's the problem (Isa. 5:2)? How would you characterize God's argument in response (Isa. 5:3–4)? What words drive home his actions in response (Isa. 5:5–6)?

7. How might Isaiah's summary of this vineyard parable (Isa. 5:7) take us back to Isaiah 1:27?

DAY FOUR—SIX WOES (ISAIAH 5:8–30)

Isaiah 5:8–30 is clearly organized; Isaiah is no ranting prophet but truly shows us the Lord's call to come and reason together. Logically following the dire vineyard verdict, these verses consist of six "Woe" sections and four "Therefore" sections. The "Therefore" sections are important for their indication of the exile to come and the divine direction of other nations to punish and purify God's sinful people.

1. Read these verses, identifying six main "Woe" sections and two pairs of "Therefore" subsections as you go. (In each case the second "Therefore" is longer and larger in scope.)

2. Make an outline or just a list of sections, giving each section a title that gets at the main idea of that section.

3. Finally, identify which "Woe" sections speak to you most personally, and why. Throughout, we must be struck with the ways in which all people, both then and now, need a redeemer to save us from our sin.

(Continued from previous page)

(Continued from previous page)

Day Five—Conclusions

1. We have covered a large portion! In these chapters we have seen the rhythm of light and dark, salvation and judgment, which will characterize the entire book. Look back through chapters 2–5, focusing on the person of God—what we learn of him, his attributes, and his ways of dealing with human beings. Write down several aspects of God that stand out to you, and then write a personal response—which could be in the form of a prayer, or questions, or simply a few sentences responding to the Lord God who speaks to us through the inspired words of this prophet who lived so long ago.

2. Look once more through the chapters and choose a verse or a short passage to write out and commit to memory. Be ready to share with your group the ways in which you find this verse or verses challenging, helpful, beautiful, etc.

Notes for Lesson 3

Lesson 4 (Isaiah 6)
THE LORD'S CALL TO ISAIAH

DAY ONE—SEEING THE HOLY ONE (ISAIAH 6:1–4)

1. Read through Isaiah 6, jotting down initial thoughts and observations.

2. What difference does it make to come to this chapter in the context of the whole book and with the perspective established by the Preface in chapters 1–5?

3. Compare and contrast the two kings of Isaiah 6:1. (Recall 2 Chronicles 26.)

4. Isaiah has already called God the "Holy One of Israel," but here he tells of encountering this holiness personally. Not all the details are explainable, but what do the various words and phrases of Isaiah 6:2–4 suggest about

the holiness of God? *Note 1: The "seraphim" are literally "burning ones." Note 2: Normally, Hebrew uses one repetition to express a superlative.*

5. Such glimpses in Scripture remind us of the heavenly reality which, though invisible, surrounds and pervades all our earthly existence. Stop and see and hear and feel this scene one more time. What might it make you pray?

DAY TWO—LOST AND SAVED (ISAIAH 6:5–7)

1. After all the cries of "Woe" in previous chapters, we
   arrive at Isaiah's personal cry in Isaiah 6:5. Examine the
   phrases of his response in this verse. What stands out
   to you, and why?

2. Why are the *lips* the focus of uncleanness here? Before
   you write anything, consider the context of this story
   with the seraphim, the context of Isaiah's prophecy, and
   the larger biblical context (for example, read Isa. 29:13;
   Matt. 15:7–9; Heb. 13:15).

3. How much do you and people around you in the church today share this response to God's holiness? Explain.

4. The Lord does not leave Isaiah lost. Think about the burning coal brought to him in Isaiah 6:6–7. What details help us understand the coal's efficacy? (See Ex. 29:35–46 and Lev. 17:11.) What does the seraph accomplish in touching the coal to Isaiah's lips? *Note: "Atoned for" literally means "covered."*

5. Return for a moment to the huge promises in Isaiah 1:18, 27. These promises grow in meaning throughout the whole book. How does Isaiah 6 enlarge our understanding of the promised cleansing and redemption?

DAY THREE—COMMISSIONED (ISAIAH 6:8–12)

1. Isaiah is now ready and able to hear (and answer!) God's call to serve (Isa. 6:8). Take a moment to read through Psalm 51. What similar process do you notice?

2. Consider the question and answer in Isaiah 6:8. How would you describe Isaiah's response? On what is it based and not based?

3. Read Isaiah 6:9–10, and then read Matthew 13:10–17 and Acts 28:17–28.

   a. What is the main point of these verses, and why is this point so important for us to understand?

b. How should these verses affect us as both *hearers* and *proclaimers* of the Word of God?

4. In Isaiah 6:11–12, what insights about Isaiah and God can we gain from this question and this part of God's answer?

DAY FOUR—A STUMP REMAINS (ISAIAH 6:13)

1. How does the picture in Isaiah 6:13 effectively follow the previous verses? What do we see and understand from this picture? *Note: a terebinth or oak tree can be felled or burned and still send out new shoots from a remaining stump.*

2. How has the book so far prepared us for Isaiah 6:13? Consider, for example, Isaiah 1:9; 1:25; 4:2–3.

3. In examining the branch of Isaiah 4:2, we looked ahead
   to Isaiah 11:1–10. Read those verses once again, this time
   looking for the stump. What do you learn?

4. Isaiah 6:13 talks about a holy "seed" or "offspring" as
   the stump. Trace God's promise of a seed or offspring
   through the following verses:

   a.   Genesis 3:15

   b.   Genesis 22:15–18

c. 2 Samuel 7:12–17

d. Matthew 1:1–17; Luke 1:68–75

5. One more question: whom did Isaiah see? Read John 12:36–43. Whose glory does John say Isaiah saw, and of whom does John say Isaiah spoke? Comment on this passage and its connection to Isaiah 6.

Day Five—Conclusions

I. What a magnificent chapter we have studied! Look back through chapter 6, focusing on the person of God—what we learn of him, his attributes, and his way of dealing with human beings. Write down several aspects of God that stand out to you, and then write your personal response—which could be in the form of a prayer, or questions, or simply a few sentences responding to the Lord God who speaks to us through the inspired words of this prophet who lived so long ago.

2. Look once more through the section and choose a verse or a short passage to write out and commit to memory. Be ready to share with your group the ways in which you find this verse or verses challenging, helpful, beautiful, etc.

Notes for Lesson 4

Lesson 5 (Isaiah 7:1–9:7)

THE LORD GIVES A SIGN

Isaiah 7 moves from the death of Uzziah (around 740 B.C.) to a time of crisis during the reign of Ahaz, around 735 B.C. The Assyrian Empire was on the rise and Israel (the northern kingdom) was afraid. So was its neighbor Syria. They made an alliance against Assyria and demanded that Judah join them, but Judah refused. So King Rezin of Syria and King Pekah of Israel threatened war against King Ahaz of Judah. Ahaz, who represents the kingly line of David, was scared to death. He even looked to Assyria for help (see 2 Kings 16:1–9). That's the context as we plunge in to the world of these little kings, right after seeing the King of Heaven in chapter 6.

DAY ONE—WHAT KIND OF A KING? (ISAIAH 7:1–9)

1. Skim Isaiah 7–8, jotting down observations and thoughts.

2. Consider Isaiah 7:1–9.

    a.   What aims are Rezin and Pekah trying to accomplish, and why will they not succeed?

    b.   Contrast Ahaz's perspective and God's perspective on these two kings.

3. In Isaiah 7:1–9, what gifts does God send to King Ahaz through the prophet Isaiah—by words and by other means? *Note 1: Damascus (Syria's capital) fell to Assyria in 732 B.C. Samaria (Israel's capital) fell to Assyria in 722 B.C., and its people*

were eventually exiled and dispersed, never again to reunite. Note 2: Shear-jashub means "A remnant shall return."

4. The last two lines of Isaiah 7:9 are God's "clincher," a rhyming wordplay in the Hebrew. Comment on these words, considering questions such as: What *is* "faith," which God evidently considers so crucial (see Heb. 11:1–2)? What in the book so far has clarified the necessity of faith? How have you experienced the truth of this potent little maxim?

DAY TWO—READING THE SIGN (ISAIAH 7:10–25)

1. God does not hide from us in order to make faith difficult. In fact, what do we see in the various phrases of Isaiah 7:10–11 that indicate quite the contrary?

2. Ahaz's first recorded words, in Isaiah 7:12, sound pious and full of faith (see Deut. 6:16–19). Why are they *not*?

3. In Isaiah 7:13, why do you think Isaiah refers to King Ahaz and to God the way he does (see also Isa. 7:2)?

4. Read Isaiah 7:14–17. *Note: The word for "virgin" here refers most commonly to an unmarried woman, a maiden, with the literal meaning of "virgin" implied.*

    a.   What words would you use to describe God as we see him in these verses? Explain briefly.

    b.   What does Matthew 1:18–25 tell us about these verses?

There may also have been an Immanuel born in Isaiah's time, as an immediate and part fulfillment of this prophecy, but in both cases it would be true, as Isaiah 7:15–17 states, that long before the boy would grow to maturity, Israel and Syria—and Judah as well—will have suffered great destruction (Assyria helped Judah against Rezin and Pekah, and then not only destroyed Syria and Israel but devastated a great portion of Judah as well). The sign is associated with judgment as well as hope.

5. In Isaiah 7:18–25, what do you notice about the way Isaiah foretells the destruction Assyria will bring? What do these images communicate? What words do you find repeated, and how are they effective?

DAY THREE—WATCH OUT FOR ASSYRIA (ISAIAH 8)

1. With the additional son of Isaiah in Isaiah 8:1–4, what message is God reiterating, and how does he make the message especially vivid? *Note 1: Maher-shalal-hash-baz means "the spoil speeds, the prey hastens." Note 2: The prophetess of v. 3 is Isaiah's wife, perhaps also a messenger of God's word—in any case one who carried and delivered the word of God to his people. This second son brings a prophecy we have already heard—but this time an immediate one.*

2. What two kinds of water are contrasted in Isaiah 8:5–8, and what does each picture? How does the second image change into another ominous picture? (Shiloah was the water source for Jerusalem.)

3. How amazing that Isaiah in v. 8 addresses God's people as "Immanuel," identifying them with the particular child to come. What hope is revealed to them in Isaiah 8:8, 9–10? (The last two verses offer a poetic address to Syria and Israel, and perhaps to all peoples and nations that rise up against God's people and try to put someone else on the throne of David.)

4. In this chapter's final section, Isaiah 8:11–22, Isaiah commits himself to following and serving God, as opposed to following the godless ones all around him. *Note: The "teaching" and the "testimony" refer to the Word of God.*

   a. What does this passage show to be the strength of the godly in the midst of much ungodliness?

   b. How will the godless often respond to the godly in their midst?

   c. In what ways do these verses challenge you personally?

Day Four—Light Shining (Isaiah 9:1–7)

1. Read through Isaiah 9:1–7. How would you characterize the transition from chapter 8 to chapter 9? *Note 1: Zebulun and Naphtali were <u>northern</u> regions, first to be invaded by enemies. The "way of the sea" is <u>west</u> toward the Mediterranean, stretching along its shores. "Beyond the Jordan" is <u>east</u>. Judah, then, will stretch in all directions, as the whole earth will become part of this latter-day picture (recall Isa. 2:2). Note 2: When referring to future events as certain as if they had already happened, Hebrew writers sometimes used verbs in the past tense, as here. Note 3: The "day of Midian" refers to Gideon's story in Judges 7.*

2. What is the main sense of this poem, as found in Isaiah 9:1–3? To what key or repeated words would you point?

3. What two similar reasons are given in Isaiah 9:4 and 9:5?

4. Read Isaiah 9:6–7, where a third and ultimate reason (the third "For") is given.

   a. What words and ideas in these verses recall words and ideas previously encountered in this book?

   b. What kind of a figure is presented here, as far as his main role is concerned? What distinguishes him in this role? What would this role have meant to the people of Isaiah's day?

c.   This son will also have a name—or names! What aspects of this promised one do the four names in Isaiah 9:6 unfold?

5. This poem tells us what the reign of the Messiah *is* like, for he has come, and he reigns. How does Matthew 4:12–25 in various and specific ways show us the king of Isaiah 9:1–7?

6. Let us not overlook the final statement of Isaiah 9:7. What do you observe about "the zeal of the LORD" in the following verses: Isaiah 37:32; 42:13; 59:15–20?

DAY FIVE—CONCLUSIONS

1. This first portion of the body of the book has shown us sinful, inadequate kings, and the promised child/King to come. The details are not yet clear, and yet they point irresistibly ahead to the one in whom all these promises are fulfilled. Look back through these chapters, focusing on the King of heaven who planned all this from the beginning. What do we learn here of God, his attributes, and his way of dealing with human beings? Write down several aspects of God that stand out to you, and then write your personal response—which could be in the form of a prayer, or questions, or simply a few sentences responding to the Lord God who speaks to us through the inspired words of this prophet who lived so long ago.

2. Look once more through the section and choose a verse or a short passage to write out and commit to memory. Be ready to share with your group the ways in which you find this verse or verses challenging, helpful, beautiful, etc.

Notes for Lesson 5

Lesson 6 (Isaiah 9:8–12:6)

THE LORD FELLS THE TREE
AND SAVES A BRANCH

DAY ONE—FOCUS ON ISRAEL (ISAIAH 9:8–10:4)

God's message of judgment to Judah becomes linked with his message to Israel, as Isaiah never loses sight of the fact that the northern kingdom of Israel (sometimes called Ephraim, using its largest tribal area to refer to the whole) also represents the seed of Abraham. Israel has turned its back on the line of David, and in this section God speaks straight to this northern kingdom which has allied itself with Syria against Assyria and against the southern kingdom of Judah.

1. Read Isaiah 9:8–10:4. Find the refrain that appears four times, concluding four sections. What is the effect of its repetition?

2. Construct a simple outline of the four sections, giving each one a summary sentence that gets at the central idea.

3. This passage echoes previous sections in which Judah and Jerusalem are condemned. For example, compare Isaiah 3:1–15 with Isaiah 9:8–10:4. What similarities and what differences do you notice?

4. How can a passage such as this one help adjust our perspectives now as God's people?

DAY TWO—ASSYRIA'S TURN
(ISAIAH 10:5–19, 24–34)

1. The focus turns to Assyria, which God will use to devastate Israel and almost devastate Judah—up to her neck, we recall. In Isaiah 10:5–15, what is God's perspective on Assyria, and what is Assyria's perspective on Assyria? Refer to specific words and verses in your answer. *Note: The cities in v. 9 were all conquered by Assyria.*

2. In Isaiah 10:5–15, note the images of rod and staff. What do these images communicate, and how do they grow in meaning through the passage?

3. Read Isaiah 10:16–19 to see what God will do to Assyria's "glory."

   a. What names of God do you find, and how are they appropriate at this point?

   b. What images portray the Lord's devastation of Assyria? Describe the pictures in your mind as you read this.

4. Isaiah 10:28–32 envisions Assyria's offensive march south toward Jerusalem, mentioning cities along the way. Nob is the last one, in sight of Jerusalem. However, this frightening description is embedded in two passages of encouragement:

   a. What two historical parallels does Isaiah draw in Isaiah 10:24–27 (see Exodus 14 and Judges 7), and how are they similarly encouraging?

   b. Isaiah 10:33–34 compares Assyria to the huge Forest of Lebanon. How is this picture effective, especially as it connects with and develops previous pictures?

5. Consider how this passage deepens our perspective on history and on the God of history. Read Psalm 2. How does this psalm further unfold God's place and purposes in the course of human events? How does the psalmist (and how do you) respond?

DAY THREE—BUT WHAT IS THE HOPE? (ISAIAH 10:20–23; 11:1–10)

1. In the "sandwiched" section of Isaiah 10:20–23, what words would you point to in order to show the nature of the hope expressed? Explain.

2. Of course we have taken these sections out of order. Read through Isaiah 10:5–11:10. What do you notice about the order of the sections and the effect of that order?

3. We have several times looked ahead to Isaiah 11:1–10. Reflect on the way in which Isaiah has prepared us for it. Now we are ready to look more closely.

    a. As this passage looks ahead to "that day" (review Lesson Three, Day One), with what words does Isaiah refer to the figure at the center (Isa. 11:1, 10)? How do these words connect to Isaiah 6:13?

b. In Isaiah 11:1–2, what do you observe concerning the role of the Spirit in this "branch"? (Read also Matt. 1:18; 3:16–4:1.)

4. In Isaiah 11:1–5, the earlier promises (for example in Isa. 1:27–28) take personal form. How would you summarize the attributes and rule of the one described here? What stands out to you in these verses?

5. In Isaiah 11:6–10, what do you observe concerning the astounding scope and effects of his rule? (Recall Isa. 2:1–4.) What words and phrases stand out, and why?

For reflection: The kingdom brought by Christ is not yet consummated, but it is here! The signal of Isaiah 11:10 has been raised (see John 12:32). How should this king's rule be evident among his people even now?

DAY FOUR—MORE LOOKING FAR AHEAD (ISAIAH 11:11–12:6)

1. Read Isaiah 11:11–16. Examine this passage to discern some of the ways it combines visions of God's deliverance in the past, in the relatively close future after the exile, and in the far future. What is the main point and effect of this passage?

2. Just as Moses sang a song after the Red Sea crossing, so Isaiah sings here—a glorious song which concludes this portion of Isaiah. How does Isaiah 12:1–2 clarify the ultimate meaning of the deliverance just described? What is being celebrated here?

3. How do both the picture and the thoughts of Isaiah
   12:3–4 seem to expand the celebration? *Note: "You" in v. 1
   is singular; "you" in vv. 3–4 is plural.*

4. How does the response to God's deliverance grow throughout
   this chapter? What happens in Isaiah 12:5–6? Read the
   chapter in its entirety, aloud if you can.

5. To what extent do you share in the emotions of this song?
   Do people hear this song from you, or from the people
   of God of whom you are a part? Why or why not? How
   can we sing this song more clearly?

DAY FIVE—CONCLUSIONS

1. As God's judgment has taken sharper focus in this weighty section, so have his mercy and grace. Look back through Isaiah 9:8–12:6, focusing on the God who revealed himself so clearly so long ago. What do we learn of him, his attributes, and his way of dealing with human beings? Write down several aspects of God that stand out to you, and then write your personal response—which could be in the form of a prayer, or questions, or simply a few sentences responding to the Lord God who speaks to us through the inspired words of this prophet.

2. Look once more through the section and choose a verse or a short passage to write out and commit to memory. Be ready to share with your group the ways in which you find this verse or verses challenging, helpful, beautiful, etc.

Notes for Lesson 6

Lesson 7 (Isaiah 13–18)

THE LORD'S HAND ON
ALL THE NATIONS I

DAY ONE—WHY ORACLES? (ISAIAH 13:1–16)

1. In Isaiah 13–23, the prophetic message is funneled into the shape of "oracles": weighty messages from God, given not just to his people but to many nations. Isaiah has prepared us for this. Mention one or two passages we have seen so far that show God's relation to all the nations.

2. These oracles contain announcements of judgment to come in various future layers: in Isaiah's time, in the time not long after Isaiah, and in the "latter days." Sometimes these layers are intertwined, but Isaiah 13:1–16 offers a relatively clear view of the end of the latter days: "the day of the Lord." What is the main point in these verses, and why do you think Isaiah begins the section with this main point?

3. It is easy to focus on the experience of the judged in such passages. But how do various phrases in Isaiah 13:1–16 turn our focus and understanding to the one judging?

4. What of this "signal" in Isaiah 13:2? What does it make you picture or understand? (See also Isaiah 5:26; 11:10, 12; 18:3.)

5. The starting point is Babylon, but this passage travels far! What words and phrases reveal the scope of the judgment foretold in 13:1–16, in relation to both people and places?

6. Skim 2 Peter 3, which also speaks of the day of the Lord. What similarities do you notice? What does Peter tell us about how God's people should live in light of that day?

DAY TWO—THE ORACLE CONCERNING
BABYLON/ASSYRIA (ISAIAH 13:17–14:27)

This first oracle continues to address Babylon on several levels: 1) as the most valued city of the Assyrian Empire (and so the oracle treats Assyria as well); 2) as the powerful center of the Babylonian Empire to come; 3) as a symbol of all those who rebel against God. Babylon, from the time of the Tower of Babel through the book of Revelation, pictures a place of defiance against the Lord.

1. The Medes (Isa. 13:17) joined Babylon in the conquest of Assyria (around 610 B.C.), but later joined the Persians (539 B.C.) in the conquest of Babylon, after which Babylon dramatically declined. What can we learn about the fate of Babylon in Isaiah 13:17–22? What details stand out?

All the desolation would be impossible to digest without the framework of mercy that Isaiah weaves into the text. The point of Isaiah 14:1–4 is that the oppressors of God's people will be brought down, and God's people will be lifted up and settled in their land. This may refer partly to the return from exile and partly to an even more distant future hope. In any case, it is significant that a traditional victory song is to be sung by God's restored people who will see his perfect justice. It is also significant, in this first part of Isaiah, that this should be a song against a proud, evil king.

2. In Isaiah 14:4–21, what words and phrases show us *how* and *how high* this evil king reaches?

3. How do these verses paint several pictures of the depths to which this king will be brought, especially in relation to other kings? *Note: "Sheol" is the realm of the dead, pictured imaginatively here.*

4. Isaiah 14:22–27 sort of "sweeps up" after this mess of destruction. As the Lord steps in and speaks, what main truth does he want us to see and understand? What words make this truth especially vivid?

5. How does (or how should) the truth of Isaiah 14:24–27 affect our perspective on our own lives and times?

DAY THREE—ORACLES CONCERNING PHILISTIA AND MOAB (ISAIAH 14:28–16:14)

1. Isaiah 14:28–32 addresses Philistia, a country enjoying only temporary relief from oppression. (The "rod" of v. 29 might be Assyria or Judah; King David had destroyed the Philistines in battle centuries earlier.)

In any case, Assyria is coming from the north! In contrast with Judah's remnant, what is true of the remnants of Babylon (Isa. 14:21–22) and Philistia (Isa. 14:29–31)?

2. The Philistines asked Judah to ally with them against Assyria. Isaiah has some counsel about how to answer. What is the basic principle involved in Isaiah's words to his people, in Isaiah 14:32?

3. The oracle concerning Moab (descendants of Lot, Abraham's nephew) gives us broadened insight into God's heart. His holy wrath and judgment come to us along with other holy qualities. What do you observe about the tone and substance of God's words in Isaiah 15:1–9 and 16:6–14? (These are verses filled with names

of Moabite cities and places—almost a map of Moabites fleeing their horrible fate.)

4. In Isaiah 16:1–2, the Moabites are pictured fleeing as fugitives westward to Judah, sending ahead the tribute of a lamb.

   a. How are God's people to respond to these outcasts, according to Isaiah 16:3–4?

   b. Page briefly through the book of Ruth. What connections do you find?

   c. What is the future hope presented in Isaiah 16:5, and how does it shine light even into the suffering of which Isaiah speaks?

5. How might this glimpse through the Moabites into the compassionate heart of God help shape us even now, as God's people?

<h2 align="center">DAY FOUR—ORACLES CONCERNING DAMASCUS AND EPHRAIM (ISAIAH 17:1–18:7)</h2>

1. Damascus (capital of Syria) and Ephraim (the northern kingdom of Israel) are intertwined in this oracle, for they were allies against Assyria and even against Judah (cf. Isaiah 7). Read Isaiah 17:1–11.

   a. Picture the progression of images offered in these verses. How might the people in Isaiah's time have grasped them even more vividly? What do these pictures communicate?

b. What brief signs of hope break through?

c. How do various names for God play a crucial role in these verses?

2. The lens is now opened even wider, to reveal a larger picture of many and distant nations. First, in Isaiah 17:12–14, how is the fearful power of the world's nations

evoked? In these same verses, however, how is that power exposed from another perspective?

3. Read Isaiah 18:1–7, in which the perspective stretches beyond Cush (present-day Ethiopia), and even farther, to a remote and foreign people . . . but can all this far-reaching extend beyond the hand of God?

   a. How is God vividly portrayed in Isaiah 18:3–6? What attributes emerge here?

   b. According to Isaiah 18:7, what part will these foreign nations play in God's clear purpose?

4. In a world of powerful and oppressed and conflicting nations, in what ways can we as God's people be challenged and encouraged by this week's passages from Isaiah?

DAY FIVE—CONCLUSIONS

1. Who is this God, who can send his oracles to all the nations of the world? This is a dense and challenging section of Isaiah, but oh how it reveals our Lord God to us! Look back through chapters 13–18, focusing on the one who rules all the nations of the world, and asking what we learn of him, his attributes, and his way of dealing with human beings. Write down several aspects of God that stand out to you, and then write a personal response—which could be in the form of a prayer, or questions, or simply a few sentences responding to the Lord God who speaks to us through the inspired words of this prophet.

2. Look once more through the chapters and choose a verse or a short passage to write out and commit to memory. Be ready to share with your group the ways in which you find the verse or verses challenging, helpful, beautiful, etc.

Notes for Lesson 7

Lesson 8 (Isaiah 19–23)

THE LORD'S HAND ON
ALL THE NATIONS II

The oracles continue, offering more glimpses into God's patterning of human history according to his perfect justice and his perfect plan of redemption, increasing insight into what God loves and hates, and growing perspective on the joy of obeying him and the desolation brought by rebellion against him.

DAY ONE—ORACLE CONCERNING
EGYPT (ISAIAH 19–20)

1. In this progression of oracles (Isaiah 13–23), we come to Egypt. Think for a moment about Egypt, with its history of magicians, sorcerers, idolatry, potent pharaohs, and high civilization. According to Isaiah 19:11–15, how would you diagnose Egypt's problem?

2. Read Isaiah 19:1–17. How are God's actions portrayed? (See also Ps. 18:6–19.)

3. The devastation described in Isaiah 19:1–15 could be associated with Assyrian invasions and/or invasions and droughts that weakened Egypt throughout subsequent centuries. In any case, what layers of social disintegration do you find in this amazing portrayal of a whole society's collapse?

4. But consider what happens in Isaiah 19:16–25.

   a. Read these verses, marking the repeated phrase that begins each of the five sections. How far might we see these verses reaching?

b. What kind of "healing" will the "striking" eventually bring to Egypt? How might these verses connect with Isaiah 2:1–5 and Revelation 5:5–14?

5. Read Isaiah 20. Here the oracle refocuses to a specific time in history—specifically the Assyrian King Sargon's conquest, which destroyed the rebellious Philistine city of Ashdod in 711 B.C. (Ashdod had vainly depended on Egypt for help). Around that time, as we shall see in the story of King Hezekiah, the people of Judah were leaning toward trusting Egypt (ruled for a time by Cush) to help them against Assyria's onslaught. What did Isaiah do (for three years!), and what was his point, or *God's* point?

DAY TWO—ORACLES CONCERNING BABYLON, DUMAH, ARABIA (ISAIAH 21)

This oracle to Babylon may start a new cycle of oracles in the text, a cycle even more mysterious and surreal to read. Babylon was devastated by the Assyrian Sennacherib in 689 B.C. This may be the fall predicted in Isaiah 21:1–10, although there were other risings and fallings to come. The perspective in this oracle comes from among God's people, whom Isaiah imagines as hearing of Babylon's fall and witnessing the relentless onslaught of Assyria. Babylon's famous "Land of the Sea" (its southern Persian Gulf region) will be, ironically, only a "wilderness of the sea" (21:1).

1. Read the dramatic, tense oracle in Isaiah 21:1–10.

   a. Describe the prophet's reaction to his vision.

   b. What is Isaiah trying to teach his people about how to see (and not to see)?

c. What vivid details stand out in the text?

2. Read Isaiah 21:11–12. *Note: Dumah (which means "silence") is a place in Edom, a nation east of Judah, which was conquered by Assyria. Seir is another name for Edom.*

    a. How would you describe this passage to someone about to read it?

    b. How does this dramatic vignette offer a very human picture of what it means to wait in the dark? How does the context of the whole book shed light on this little scene and on all our times of waiting?

3. God speaks and sees even into the hidden places of the desert. The Assyrian oppression reached all the way to the nomadic tribes of Arabia (Kedar). Those near an oasis (such as Dedan and Tema) are told to give aid. What is the general and final tone of this oracle in Isaiah 21:13–17?

DAY THREE—ORACLE CONCERNING JERUSALEM (ISAIAH 22)

1. This oracle refers centrally to the time of the Assyrian Sennacherib's invasion of Judah (to the gates of King Hezekiah's Jerusalem) in 701 B.C., but perhaps also to the fall of Jerusalem to Babylon in 586 B.C. Read through Isaiah 22, and then peek ahead at Hezekiah's story as told in 2 Chronicles 32, jotting down initial comments and observations.

2. What insights does Isaiah 22:1–14 give us about the minds and hearts of Jerusalem's people?

3. What are your thoughts on this "valley of vision" in Isaiah 22:1, 5? What other references to *seeing* do you find in Isaiah 22:1–14?

4. Two men serving under King Hezekiah illustrate the different outcomes of blindness and vision: *Shebna* (who was once steward over the king's household) and *Eliakim* (who replaced Shebna; see Isa. 36:1–3). Read Isaiah 22:15–19. What was Shebna's wrong, and how is the vivid judgment appropriately pictured?

5. In Isaiah 22:20–24, "In that day" marks a look ahead to Eliakim.

   a. What phrases and pictures emphasize his special designation and honor?

   b. And yet, what do we see in Isaiah 22:25? How does this verse lead us to keep looking ahead, in regard to this house of David?

DAY FOUR—ORACLE CONCERNING TYRE AND SIDON (ISAIAH 23)

Tyre and Sidon were the great port cities of Phoenicia on the Mediterranean Sea, known for their flourishing commerce and decadent lifestyles. Egypt especially, along with all the countries in the region, depended on these ports, which regularly welcomed the ships of Tarshish (huge merchant vessels). The Assyrians devastated these cities around 701 B.C.

1. In Isaiah 23:1–14, what perspectives are we given on the fall of Tyre and Sidon?

2. In what ways might Isaiah 23, as well as Isaiah 22, cause us to reflect on the nations of our day?

3. "In that day," according to Isaiah 23:15, a renewal would come to Tyre. This may mean Tyre's revitalization, which happened as the Assyrian Empire declined, or it may reach out much farther in time.

   a. Read 23:15–18. Although a bit unclear, what sort of hope is offered here?

b. What helpful perspective might we find in Ezra 3:1–7, which describes the rebuilding that took place after the return from exile?

c. What further helpful perspective might we find in Psalm 87, which anticipates those latter days of Isaiah 2?

DAY FIVE—CONCLUSIONS

1. We have come through the oracles! The weight of them is indeed something we should feel, especially in our busy, materialistic, pleasure-oriented world. True redemptive hope emerges from true darkness and grows from looking up in the midst of darkness to the one true God. Look back through chapters 19–23, focusing on the God who reveals himself clearly even in the darkness of these passages. What do we learn of him, his attributes, and his

way of dealing with human beings? Write down several aspects of God that stand out to you, and then write your own response to the Lord God who speaks to us through the inspired words of this prophet.

2. Look once more through the section and choose a verse or a short passage to write out and commit to memory. Be ready to share with your group the ways in which you find the verse or verses challenging, helpful, beautiful, etc.

Notes for Lesson 8

Lesson 9 (Isaiah 24–27)

THE LORD DESTROYS ONE CITY AND SAVES ANOTHER

God's judgment and his salvation—which Isaiah has unfolded from the beginning, and which he has turned toward particular nations in the oracles (chapters 13–23)—now dramatically expand to encompass the whole earth for all time.

DAY ONE—THE WASTED CITY (ISAIAH 24)

1. Isaiah 24 brings us to a dramatic picture of God's coming judgment. In Isaiah 24:1–6, what things can we observe about that judgment? What is the effect of the patterned and repeated words?

2. Consider Isaiah 24:5–6, which might first make us look
   back rather than ahead. Read also Genesis 3:14–19;
   9:8–17; 2 Samuel 23:1–7; Psalm 105:7–10. What connections might you notice? *Note: "Few men are left" (Isa. 24:6)
   uses the Hebrew word often translated "remnant."*

3. In one sentence, how would you describe the picture
   Isaiah paints in order to portray this curse-devoured
   earth (Is. 24:7–13)? What details stand out? *Note: The
   Hebrew word for "wasted" in Isaiah 24:10 is translated "without form"
   in Genesis 1:2.*

4. A song breaks in over this desolate scene, in Isaiah 24:14–16. From where does it come, and what emotions fill this song? How is the hero of this song named and described? What *is* this song?

5. But Isaiah reminds us that we are not there yet. How does Isaiah 24:16–23 pull us back to the chapter's earlier themes? What words and pictures stand out?

DAY TWO—THE SONG BREAKS THROUGH (ISAIAH 25)

After the dark opening movement of chapter 24, the music indeed changes. The song that was echoing around the edges breaks through and takes over—with several different movements in these next chapters!

1. In Isaiah 25:1–5, what is the place of devastation and what is the place of hope? What aspects of God are celebrated here?

2. What three-word phrase, repeated three times in Isaiah 25:6–11, tells us the place from which this song is sung? What do we know about the place from our study of Isaiah?

3. This place is all about the one at the center of it. Revel in this revelation of the Lord God in Isaiah 25:6−9. What observations about him can you make?

4. How could we not turn to Revelation 19:6−9 and 21:1−4? How do these verses "match" and deepen Isaiah 25:6−9?

5. We do not always continue reading, in Revelation 21:5−8. How do those verses "match" and deepen Isaiah 25:10−12 (where Moab stands for all the unbelieving peoples)?

6. Note the "hands" in Isaiah 25:10–12. How do these pictures work? What can we learn from them?

DAY THREE—SINGING IN THE CITY (ISAIAH 26)

In contrast with that wasted, broken-down city of Isaiah 24, here we see the lasting city. As we enter it, we enter the minds and hearts of God's faithful people, for Isaiah 26 is the song of those who trust in the Lord. Listening to the song they will sing "in that day," we find we can begin to sing it now. Read Isaiah 26 in its entirety first.

1. In Isaiah 26:1–4, what phrases show God's role and what phrases show the people's part in this climactic celebration of the city?

2. Isaiah 26:3 is a key verse.

   a. How is it different from the verses around it?

   b. Looking at this "perfect peace" (literally "peace, peace")
       in the context of these verses and this book, how
       would you define it?

   c. What hinders this peace in God's people—or in you?
       What helps us receive it as God's gift?

3. The city God establishes is contrasted with the "lofty city" that will be ruined. Why is Isaiah 26:5–6 a logical and important part of this song?

4. How does the beautiful prayer of Isaiah 26:7–9 evidence both the security and the yearning of God's trusting people on the way to this city? What is the repeated focus of their yearning? How might this challenge us?

5. How is "the path of your judgments" (Isa. 26:8) more fully explained in Isaiah 26:9–11? What is good about this path?

6. Read Isaiah 26:12–19, and then meditate on Isaiah 26:12.

   a. How is God contrasted with other lords and rulers (Isa. 26:13–15)?

   b. How is God starkly contrasted with his feeble people (Isa. 26:16–18)?

c.   What is the amazing hope of Isaiah 26:19? Find this hope also in Job 19:25–27 and Ezekiel 37:11–14.

d.   How is the huge truth of Isaiah 26:12 enriched by the context of this passage—and this chapter—and this book?

7. Finally, how does Genesis 7:15–16 relate to Isaiah 26:20–21? What do we learn here?

The Lord Destroys One City and Saves Another

DAY FOUR—LOOKING AHEAD
TO REDEMPTION (ISAIAH 27)

This vision of the end in chapters 24–27 comes to a climax here with one unbelievably moving solo, which then grows to a triumphant, trumpeting finale. To see the shape of chapter 27, look through and find the two opening and the two closing "In that day" phrases. We are looking far, far ahead here.

1. The first "In that day" summarizes the final destruction of evil, pictured here in the form of a sea monster called "Leviathan." Read Isaiah 27:1 (and Rev. 12:1–9 for further identification of this dragon figure). What details of his fate stand out to you in this first, violent verse?

2. With another layer of "In that day," a sudden calm emerges in Isaiah 27:2–6.

   a. How does this song contrast with the previous vineyard song, in Isaiah 5:1–7?

b. What characteristics of this keeper/singer emerge here?

c. How big will this vineyard be? How does this connect with previous themes?

3. In Isaiah 27:7–9, in what ways do we see God's redemptive purposes and amazing mercy toward his people even in the midst of devastating judgment?

4. Chapter 27 draws to a close with two contrasting pictures:
   one, a final picture of the forsaken city, its people judged
   by God for being "without discernment" (Isa. 27:10–11).
   But what other picture finally bursts onto the scene,
   in Isaiah 27:12? *Note: This beautiful picture uses the largest
   boundaries of the Promised Land as a setting.*

5. With a final layer of "in that day," Isaiah 27:13 further expands
   this picture. End this day simply by reading and meditating
   on this magnificent verse, along with Isaiah 2:1–4; 11:12–16;
   Matthew 24:29–31; 1 Thessalonians 4:16–17.

DAY FIVE—CONCLUSIONS

1. How can we process such a huge look into what is to
   come? What *vision* Isaiah was granted! How we need such
   vision today! Do we really believe that the world God
   created is moving toward such an end, according to these
   sovereign purposes he has revealed? What difference
   should that make to us now? Look back through chapters
   24–27, focusing on the God who reveals himself clearly
   as he unveils his plans for the universe and for his people.
   What do we learn of him, his attributes, and his way
   of dealing with human beings? Write down several
   aspects of God that stand out to you, and then write

your own personal response—which could be in the form of a prayer, or questions, or simply a few sentences responding to the Lord God who has ordained the past, present, and future of our world.

2. Look once more through the section and choose a verse or a short passage to write out and commit to memory. Be ready to share with your group the ways in which you find the verse or verses challenging, helpful, beautiful, etc.

Notes for Lesson 9

Lesson 10 (*Isaiah* 28–30)

THE LORD CALLS US
TO TRUST HIM

Chapter 28 begins a new section that in effect asks God's people to place their trust in all the huge redemptive purposes we have seen so far. The historical context of chapters 28–30 is the story of Judah's good, but not wise, King Hezekiah. The king wants to run to Egypt for help against the Assyrians who, having conquered Samaria, now threaten Jerusalem. Isaiah's message in the six "Woes" or "Ahs" of chapters 28–35 is to *trust the Lord*.

DAY ONE—AH, THE PROUD
CROWN . . . (ISAIAH 28)

1. Before addressing Judah, Isaiah takes a glance back to Ephraim (the northern kingdom, whose corrupt capital Samaria was like a glittering crown on a hill). To grasp what Isaiah sees ahead for Samaria at the hand of Assyria, trace the "crown" and the "beauty" through Isaiah 28:1–6.

2. The attention turns to Judah, likewise corrupt. Read Isaiah 28:7–13.

   a. What is the people's main problem in Isaiah 28:12?

   b. What reasons do you find in Isaiah 28:7–10 for their failure to hear God's word? *Note: Isaiah 28:9–10 re-creates the mocking of Judah's leaders, who use a kind of nonsensical baby talk to imply that Isaiah's simple teaching is infantile and foolish.*

   c. What will be the outcome of not hearing God's word (Isa. 28:11–13)?

d. Do such attitudes toward God's Word continue today? How? Where?

3. Read Isaiah 28:14–22, in which Isaiah begins to preach against Judah's alliance with Egypt. In this passage, what contrasts do we find with the "everlasting covenant" of God with his people? (See Lesson Nine, Day One, question 2.)

4. How does Isaiah 28:16–17 *show* us why we should trust in the Lord and no one else? See also Psalm 118:19–23 and 1 Peter 2:4–8.

5. How does Isaiah 28:18–22 communicate the results of dependence on Egypt? *Note: In the two battles mentioned in Isaiah 28:21, the Lord acted in battle for his people, not against them.*

6. What is the main message of the two short concluding parables (Isa. 28:23–26, 27–29)? How might these parables have encouraged those in Isaiah's time—and how might they encourage us?

DAY TWO—AH, ARIEL . . . (ISAIAH 29)

1. In Isaiah 29:1–4, Isaiah alludes to the Assyrian siege of Jerusalem (called "Ariel"—the meaning of which is disputed). Who is speaking here, what is the tone (or tones), and what is the point?

2. The text moves on to picture the fate of those (Assyrians and others) whom God will use to punish Judah. In Isaiah 29:5–8, what images are at work—for what end?

3. In Isaiah 29:9–14, how does Isaiah expose the situation in Jerusalem that brings about God's judgment—and how is the judgment appropriately stated? (Recall Isaiah 6:9–13.)

4. The third "Woe" or "Ah" begins a section (Isa. 29:15–21) that shows the nature of what God will do. How would you summarize and/or outline this section?

5. The chapter's final verses develop the hope that began to grow in the previous ones. Read Isaiah 29:22–24. What are some of the beautiful transformations that God says will happen among his people? In what ways do you see some of these transformations happening even now, among God's people?

DAY THREE—AH, STUBBORN CHILDREN . . . (ISAIAH 30:1–14)

1. In Isaiah 30:1–2, how does Isaiah identify both the specific wrong he is condemning and the essence of that wrong?

2. Why do we as God's people tend toward the kind of wrong Isaiah here addresses? In what ways have you perhaps personally encountered this tendency?

3. What words work together in Isaiah 30:3–5 to communicate the results of such disobedience? *Note: Zoan and Hanes were located in Egypt.*

4. Isaiah 30:6–7 is an ironic little poem focusing on animals that carried Judah's ambassadors across the Negeb desert to Egypt, to take gifts and ask for aid. What truths ought God's people to know about Egypt, according to Isaiah 30:5–7? What in their history should offer further perspective on this trek to Egypt? *Note: "Rahab" perhaps*

refers to a Canaanite mythical monster—here a mocking nickname for Egypt.

5. Read the Lord's condemnation of his people in Isaiah 30:8–17.

   a. In what ways are *words* shown here to be of such vital importance to God?

   b. The results of despising God's word and trusting in perverseness are pictured in Isaiah 30:13–14. What do these two pictures make you see and understand?

Day Four—More of These Stubborn Children (Isaiah 30:15–33)

1. We paused in the middle of God's condemnation—at a crucial point. Read and meditate on Isaiah 30:15. How do these powerful parallel lines work together to develop what main point?

2. Read Isaiah 30:16–18. As Isaiah points ahead, in what ways do both desolation and hope emerge? What words tell us about the nature of the hope?

3. Isaiah 30:19–26 shows a God who does not withhold punishment and adversity but who delivers his people. Here we see another remarkable picture of the gathering of God's people in the final Zion. The return from

exile would foreshadow this fulfillment, and now we know this fulfillment through Christ who has come and accomplished our salvation. Yet we long for the perfect consummation of his final coming. Read these verses looking for the ways and roles in which God is portrayed, and the various kinds of responses and results he will call forth.

4. Along with final redemption, the final judgment is not left out. Read Isaiah 30:27–28 and 30–33, remembering that the Lord's "name" represents his very character and being. In this portrait of God as an awesome warrior figure, *what specific parts of God* are pictured as doing *what*? What effect does such a portrait have?

5. How amazing to find such a violent coming greeted with the glad song of Isaiah 30:29! The verse may suggest a night pilgrimage such as the people experienced during the Feast of Passover, marching together up to the temple on Mount Zion and singing psalms along the way. What is the source of the gladness here? (See also Psalm 42:4–11.)

DAY FIVE—CONCLUSIONS

1. These are very personal chapters, asking God's people to trust this God who is in charge of all of history—even when we're under siege, and even in the middle of the night. Where will we run for help? Look back through chapters 28–30, focusing on this God who, because of who he is, calls for our trust. What do we learn of him, his attributes, and his way of dealing with human beings? Write down several aspects of God that stand out to you, and then write a personal response—which could be a prayer, or questions, or simply a few sentences that express your trusting response to the Lord God who speaks to us through the inspired words of this prophet.

(Continued from previous page)

2. Look once more through these chapters and choose a verse or a short passage to write out and commit to memory. Be ready to share with your group the ways in which you find the verse or verses challenging, helpful, beautiful, etc.

Notes for Lesson 10

Lesson 11 (Isaiah 31–35)

THE LORD WILL ESTABLISH
HIS KINGDOM

Two more of the six "Woes" or "Ahs" of chapters 28–35 remain—but much more than woe is found in them. God continues to call his people to trust, still in the context of King Hezekiah's story (to come in the next lesson). These chapters proclaim not only judgment but also hope in the promised king.

DAY ONE—WOE TO THOSE WHO GO
DOWN TO EGYPT (ISAIAH 31–32)

I. The fifth "woe" begins by addressing Judah's effort to procure Egypt's help against the Assyrians, in disobedience to Isaiah's word from the Lord.

    a. How does Isaiah 31:1 effectively describe the crux of the people's sin?

b. To what aspects of God does Isaiah point (Isa. 31:2–5), in contrast with the Egyptians? What elements of the poetry here make the point especially vivid?

c. Isaiah 31:6 is the "hinge," calling for repentance in light of both what has been said and what is to come, most immediately God's judgment on Assyria. What motivations for this call to repentance do you find in Isaiah 31:6–9?

2. If Isaiah 31:6 is the hinge, then Isaiah 32:1 is the climax! Find the common qualities of this king in Isaiah 1:27; 9:7; 11:4–5; 32:1. Why are these qualities so crucial?

3. In Isaiah 32:2–5, how do the effects of such a rule answer the needs we have seen in the Judah of Isaiah's time? Even as we pray for his kingdom to come fully and finally, how and where are these effects of his rule evident today?

4. The two main figures of Isaiah 32:5–8 stand up and block our vision temporarily. How do the fool and the scoundrel live out the *opposite* of both righteousness and justice?

5. Again Isaiah focuses on the women! In Isaiah 32:9–14, how does the portrayal of these women relate to Isaiah's call to trust God? What repeated words stand out?

The verses that follow flood the end of this "Woe" with a renewed and overwhelmingly rich vision of the king's rule. Notice (Isa. 32:15) that the *Spirit's* outpouring will usher it in—the third person of the Trinity who was hovering over the face of the waters at creation, who has enlivened faith in God's people from the beginning, who filled God's chosen leaders throughout the Old Testament, who rests on the shoot from the stump of Jesse (Isa. 11:1–5), who came in new fullness as the Spirit of the risen Christ at Pentecost, and who now fills the heart of everyone who belongs to Christ the King.

6. Read Isaiah 32:15–20 slowly, relishing the pictured fruit of the Spirit. What two words were you sure to find in this section, and in what ways do they affect everything around them?

Day Two—Ah, You Destroyer! (Isaiah 33)

1. In this sixth and final "Woe," judgment on Assyria again broadens to a view of worldwide judgment—and mercy. What does Isaiah 33:1 show about the Assyrians, and how does 2 Kings 18:13–17 shed further light?

2. Isaiah 33:2–6 points toward heaven, in the midst of attack. In contrast with the plunder sought by Assyria, what kinds of treasures do these words encourage God's people to seek? How might these verses encourage and challenge you?

3. The rhythm of this chapter is familiar: one moment looking ahead with hope, and the next moment seeing desolation of all kinds. Isaiah 33:7–9 looks again to

desolation, not just of Assyria but in general, with places famous for beauty shown bare and sorrowful. How does Isaiah 33:10 stand out with dramatic effect between verses 7–9 and 11–12?

4. Read Isaiah 33:13–16, along with Exodus 19:16–20 and Hebrews 12:18–29. Write down several observations and personal responses.

5. The hope lies in the person of the king, who is the central focus in Isaiah 33:17–22. Write down everything you can learn about him and the effects of his rule. Then consider the ways these verses point to deliverance from the Assyrians, deliverance for us as God's people now, and final deliverance to come.

6. Can you identify with the picture in the first part of Isaiah 33:23? How? But then how does the remainder

of the chapter offer the most full and beautiful picture of hope to come?

DAY THREE—THE LORD HAS A DAY (ISAIAH 34)

Here the Lord's response to sin is even more fully uncovered. We have seen enough of his love and mercy so far in this book to know the inaccuracy of the stereotype of the purely wrathful Old Testament God. However, his judgment on sin is clear—and crucial to an understanding of salvation. This is an important chapter.

1. What words and phrases in Isaiah 34:1–4 communicate the breadth and depth of God's message here?

2. The Lord "has" several things in this passage: first, his rage against sin. What more does he have, in Isaiah

34:5–7, and what is communicated here? *Note: Edom, the nation of the descendants of Esau, fought against God's people for centuries, and often in Scripture represents any people who rebel against God. Bozrah was its capital.*

3. Finally, in Isaiah 34:8–10, what is emphasized, and how, concerning something else the Lord has?

4. The rest of the chapter paints a picture of a land apportioned and judged by God's own measuring lines as a wild place of *confusion* and *emptiness* (Isa. 34:11). Those two words repeat the *formless* and *empty* of Genesis 1:2. How does Isaiah 34:8–15 show the opposite of God's blessing?

5. This passage does not picture nature wildly and randomly taking over. What forces are at work, and what truths do we learn about God, in Isaiah 34:16–17?

DAY FOUR—A JOYFUL SONG! (ISAIAH 35)

After such darkness, what a glorious song bursts forth! What a picture of God's people coming into the land—reminiscent of the joyful end to the exodus, anticipating the joyful end to the exile, and ultimately looking forward to the kingdom brought by King Jesus and consummated by his final coming as both judge and king over all the nations.

1. Read and relish the entire chapter. Jot down initial comments and observations.

2. How would you divide Isaiah 35 into four sections, and how might you title them?

LESSON 11 (ISAIAH 31–35)

3. Find each mention of "LORD" or "God" in this chapter. What is his role in this picture of the joyful gathering of God's people?

4. Consider the import of the words "redeemed" and "ransomed" in Isaiah 35:9–10. What do they mean, and how are they climactic at this point in the book? How do they explain God's people being able to return with singing along the "Way of Holiness"?

5. Again we see the transforming effect of the Lord's redemption. What elements of this chapter's picture reverse the desolation in the previous chapter, or in earlier ones (for example, Isa. 6:10; 24:1–13; 33:7–9)?

6. What specifically encourages you in this chapter, as one of the redeemed?

Day Five—Conclusions

1. As the culmination of the poetry in the book's first large section, Isaiah 31–35 exalts the king and makes the effects of his rule even more vivid. How could we not trust such a king for our salvation? Look back through these chapters, focusing on the Lord God who has set his king on his holy mountain (cf. Psalm 2). What do we learn of him, his attributes, and his way of dealing with human beings?

Write down several aspects of God that stand out to you, and then write a personal response—which could be in the form of a prayer, or questions, or simply a few sentences that express your response to the Lord God who speaks to us through the inspired words of this prophet.

2. Look once more through the section and choose a verse or a short passage to write out and commit to memory. Be ready to share with your group the ways in which you find the verse or verses challenging, helpful, beautiful, etc.

Notes for Lesson 11

Lesson 12 (Isaiah 36–39)

The Lord Writes
Hezekiah's Story—
and History

We have reached what is often called a "bridge section": Chapters 36–37 of Isaiah tell the story of the Assyrian threat to Jerusalem, which has been looming behind so many of the prophetic utterances so far. Chapters 38–39 look ahead to the next focus of attention, in chapters 40–55, the Babylonian captivity. The events of chapters 38–39 most likely occurred before the events of chapters 36–37, but they are arranged thematically rather than chronologically. These prose stories stand out in the text not only because of their different style but also because they give concrete illustration of Isaiah's message concerning God's sovereign judgment and mercy, and man's need to trust such a God. Parallel passages appear in 2 Kings 18:13–20:19 and 2 Chronicles 32.

DAY ONE—SENNACHERIB AT THE GATES (ISAIAH 36:1–37:13)

1. Lesson One noted the two "attacked-king" stories that serve as bookends to this first large section lifting up the coming king (chapters 7–39). Here we are at the other end! Read Isaiah 36:1–3 and review 7:1–3, noting the parallels. *Note: The Rabshakeh was the official representative of King Sennacherib of Assyria.*

2. Isaiah 36:4–10 presents a masterful challenge to Hezekiah's men. What are the Rabshakeh's key word and key question? List and evaluate the arguments he puts forth to bring the Judeans into submission.

3. Rejecting the Jewish officials' request that the Assyrians speak in the diplomatic language of Aramaic (which would spare the gathered Jews from understanding and fear), the Rabshakeh continues his verbal attack. Analyze his speech in Isaiah 36:11–20, which presents his king's words. How does King Sennacherib view himself, Hezekiah, the people, and the Lord God? *Note this speech's key word!*

4. When Hezekiah's men bring their report (Isa. 36:21–22), what sorts of attitudes toward and beliefs about God do his actions and words show, in Isaiah 37:1–4?

Read Isaiah 37:5–9 to reaffirm which king is in charge of this story. A rumor *was* planted, concerning Tirhakah (who commanded the Egyptian troops), and so Sennacherib moved from Lachish (next to Jerusalem) north to Libnah—toward home. But before going, Sennacherib sent another threatening message to Hezekiah. Read Isaiah 37:9–13 and notice this evil king's perspective on God and gods in general.

DAY TWO—JUST AS GOD SAID
(ISAIAH 37:14–38)

1. What can we learn from Hezekiah's response to Sennacherib's repeated threats, in Isaiah 37:14?

2. With what names of and truths about God does Hezekiah begin and fill his prayer, in Isaiah 37:15–20? *Note: In the temple's Most Holy Place, hammered gold cherubim guarded either side of the mercy seat, the cover of the ark of the covenant which represented God's presence with his people—often referred to as the footstool of God on his throne.*

3. How does such a view of God affect Hezekiah's concerns and requests in this prayer?

4. What aspect of Hezekiah's prayer most challenges you as you think about your prayers?

5. God answers Hezekiah's prayer by letting him hear his word. In Isaiah 37:22–29, of what wrongs does God accuse Sennacherib?

6. In Isaiah 37:22–35, what truths about himself is God revealing? Refer to specific phrases and verses. Reread also Isaiah 14:24–27.

7. The accomplishment of God's specific promises (Isa. 37:33–35) is told in Isaiah 37:36–38. What details strike you here?

DAY THREE—A PREVIOUS SICKNESS (ISAIAH 38)

There is some discussion concerning exact dates, especially as recorded years of reigns may include some overlapping monarchies, but most agree that "In those days" (38:1) refers to a time just a few years before Sennacherib's invasion.

1. Isaiah 38:1–3 sets the scene as we move from battlefields into one man's bedroom. It is a hard moment. What do we see in Hezekiah here, especially in contrast with the previous chapters?

2. Read Isaiah 38:4–8. Then read Isaiah 38:21–22 for further details, and 2 Kings 20:1–11 for further clarification. What truths do these verses show us about God's interaction with his creatures and with his creation?

3. Hezekiah's writing appears in Isaiah 38:9–20. What words and images vividly communicate his feelings and his perspective while facing death?

4. How would you sum up what Hezekiah is saying, in Isaiah 38:15–20?

5. Hezekiah's illness was a time of either reviving or receiving faith rather than a time of meeting trouble as an already deeply faithful man. We know Hezekiah was a good king, characterized in 2 Kings 18 as one who trusted in the Lord. We have seen his faithful turning to the Lord in a time of national crisis. But now, as preparation for Isaiah 39, read 2 Chronicles 32:24–31. What

helpful insights into his heart (and perhaps yours) do you find?

DAY FOUR—HEZEKIAH FAILS THE TEST (ISAIAH 39)

Babylon at this time was under Assyrian rule but always strong and always rebelling—and always looking for partners in rebellion. Here was another potential ally for Hezekiah to trust and impress, rather than simply leaning on the promises of God for deliverance (see Isa. 38:6).

1. Read Isaiah 39:1–2. What different sort of attack does Hezekiah face here, and how would you analyze his response?

2. In Isaiah 39:3–7, what do you observe about Isaiah's response?

3. This moment connects to a much larger story. Isaiah is here foretelling the Babylonian captivity and exile of the Judean people—over a century in advance. Babylon has not even yet established an empire. Some critics have not thought this possible, wondering whether a later writer was responsible for such parts of the book. How do these verses (and indeed the message of the entire book so far) help us to process this message of Isaiah concerning times to come?

4. Comment on Hezekiah's response in Isaiah 39:8. What might be Isaiah's purpose in ending this section of the book with such a verse?

5. Think back to Isaiah 32:1–2, 17–18, and contrast that picture of "peace" and "security" with the kind Hezekiah here embraces. In what ways have you known the tensions and temptations of trying to achieve peace and security for yourself?

DAY FIVE—CONCLUSIONS

1. So far in Isaiah, we have seen earthly examples of bad kings and good kings—but none perfect, and none who can establish the kind of kingdom we have foreseen with Isaiah. He has turned our eyes to the eternal king. Isaiah compels us to look up and ahead, and that is what we will do as we study the remaining chapters. We will look forward not only to the *King*, but to the *Suffering Servant*, and to the eternal *Conqueror*—in poetry that will lift us up to see far, far ahead. For now, in conclusion to this first magnificent section, look back through Isaiah 36–39, focusing on the Lord God who deals mercifully with his needy people in order to accomplish his redemptive promises and purposes. What do we learn of him, his attributes, and his way of dealing with human beings? Write down several aspects of God that stand out to

you, and then write a personal response—which could be in the form of a prayer, or questions, or simply a few sentences responding to the Lord God who speaks to us through the inspired words of this prophet.

2. Look once more through the section and choose a verse or a short passage to write out and commit to memory. Be ready to share with your group the ways in which you find the verse or verses challenging, helpful, beautiful, etc.

Notes for Lesson 12

Lesson 13 (Isaiah 40:1-41:20)

The Lord Himself Comforts His People

Day One—Where Were We? (Isaiah 40:1-2)

With Isaiah's second section, we are not only transitioning but also *continuing* the prophetic vision introduced in the book's opening verse. In early manuscripts, what we call chapter 39 moves with no marked separation right into the text of chapter 40. This is the point where some modern critics would indicate a second author, partly because the focus shifts to a period well beyond Isaiah's lifetime. Perhaps the most helpful perspective on the authorship issue is the book's own repeated portrait of a mighty God who ordains all of history according to his redemptive purposes. The Lord's direction of history is his holy, supernatural work—as was his inspiration of Isaiah's words from beginning to end.

1. First, recall the context of *prophecy* and what it entails. Look back to Isaiah 1:1-2, 10-11, 18, 20, 24, and now read 40:1, 5.

2. Recall the context of the *writing prophets*, whose prophecies
    (words from God) were given in relation to the exile of
    God's people from their land. In Isaiah 1–39 the great
    enemy was Assyria, who took into exile the northern
    kingdom of Israel (during Isaiah's lifetime). In these
    next chapters the great enemy is Babylon, who took into
    exile the southern kingdom of Judah (a century after
    Isaiah's ministry). Look back to Isaiah 39:5–8. What
    details stand out in this account of Isaiah's prediction
    of the Babylonian captivity?

3. What observations can you make about the transition
    from Isaiah 39:5–8 to Isaiah 40:1–2?

4. We saw at the start this book's overarching shape, moving from a Jerusalem of disobedience and destruction to a New Jerusalem of renewal and communion with God. The first section pointed to the promised king who will accomplish this. Imagine the desolation of Judah's people when their kingdom was shattered and their people exiled. Consider Isaiah 40:1–2, spoken prophetically to a people whose crushed hope Isaiah foresees. How would these words minister to them? Which words stand out? *Note: "Comfort" in v. 1 is a command in the plural, addressed to a host of heaven-sent comforters whose voices we are about to hear.*

5. Read through Isaiah 40, jotting down initial thoughts and observations.

DAY TWO—THREE VOICES OF
COMFORT (ISAIAH 40:1–11)

1. The call to give comfort is obeyed first by a voice talking about a highway (Isa. 40:3–5).

   a. In Isaiah 40:3, what physical activity pictures what spiritual reality? Before answering, read in Matthew 3:1–6 what the Bible tells us is the fulfillment of this prophecy.

   b. How does Isaiah 40:4–5 develop the picture?

   c. "Glory" implies the shining forth of God's very being. Read Isaiah 4:2–6; Isaiah 40:5; John 1:14; and 2 Corinthians 4:3–6. What can you observe about God's glory?

2. Comfort comes not only from this first voice's promise; it comes also from the source and certainty of the promise. The second voice offers what physical reality to communicate what spiritual truth, in Isaiah 40:6–8?

3. Stop and ponder. How do these three verses light up your life right now, on this particular day, as you study the Scriptures?

4. The third voice urges the people of God to look up and see the Lord who will himself appear. What aspects of his coming are the people urged to announce and anticipate, in Isaiah 40:9–11?

5. Consider the ways in which these voices have brought comfort to God's people through unfolding stages of history, beginning in Isaiah's time. Perhaps they brought comfort first to Isaiah himself, as he wrote these inspired words. How does this perspective help you receive the comfort of these words?

DAY THREE—LIFT UP YOUR EYES (ISAIAH 40:12–31)

1. Read Isaiah 40:12–26. What is the central point of these magnificent verses?

2. Examine the two sets of questions in Isaiah 40:12 and Isaiah 40:13–14. What two aspects of God do they celebrate? What is the effect of these questions as you read them?

3. How do the pictures of Isaiah 40:15–17 make vivid God's relation to the *nations*? Then how does Isaiah 40:18–20 offer an appropriate response? *Note: Lebanon was known for its many forests and fine cattle.*

4. How do the pictures of Isaiah 40:21–24 effectively show God's relation to the *inhabitants* of the nations? How does Isaiah 40:25–26 offer an appropriate response?

5. Isaiah 40:27–31 brings the chapter to a beautiful climax. What wrong tendency does verse 27 address? To whom is this reproach given, and why should they know better?

6. How does Isaiah 40:27–31 correct that wrong tendency? What aspects of God and what aspects of human beings do these verses make clear?

7. Meditate on the following verses along with Isaiah 40:27–31: Isaiah 26:8; Psalm 27:14; Exodus 19:3–4. How do these verses strengthen your heart and mind?

DAY FOUR—THE LORD TELLS HIS PLANS
FOR HIS PEOPLE (ISAIAH 41:1–20)

I. God speaks here, addressing peoples as far away as the
coastlands, and in effect calling all the nations to order
for a hearing. He first mentions "one from the east"
(Isa. 41:2)—a reference to Cyrus of Persia, the future
conqueror of the Babylonians and liberator of the exiled
Jews. Cyrus will emerge more clearly in a few chapters.
Read Isaiah 41:1–7. What main point is God making
about this great conqueror? In what ways is the point
driven home effectively?

2. God's plans focus in on his people in the next three
sections. Examine the beginning verse of each section (v.
8, v. 14, and v. 17). Write down everything you can discern
about *the nature and identity of God's people* as he addresses
them in these three verses. What strikes you as you look
at what you have written?

3. In Isaiah 41:8–13, find and write down verbs. These words will tell what the Lord *has done, is doing,* and *will do* for his people. How do you respond as you look at what you have written? What response is called for in the text?

4. In Isaiah 41:14–16, what's the picture and what does it communicate? How is God's own identity (watch for the names given him) central to this passage?

5. In Isaiah 41:17–20, in what ways does Isaiah vividly portray the picture, the identity of the main character, the action, and the action's purpose?

6. In what ways do we see God now accomplishing the things spoken of in Isaiah 41:8–20? How do we participate in the accomplishment of these things?

DAY FIVE—CONCLUSIONS

1. The middle section of Isaiah looks ahead to a people suffering in exile and lifts their eyes to the Lord God who will never fail to lift up his people. These inspired words have for centuries pointed readers to look up to the Holy One of Israel, from any point of need. Look back through the passages we have read, focusing on the person of God—what we learn of him, his attributes, and his way of dealing with human beings. Write down several aspects of God that stand out to you, and then write your personal response—which could be in the form of a prayer, or questions, or simply a few sentences

responding to the Lord God who will never cease to watch over his people.

2. Look once more through the section and choose a verse or a short passage to write out and commit to memory. Be ready to share with your group the ways in which you find the verse (or verses) challenging, helpful, beautiful, etc.

Notes for Lesson 13

Lesson 14 (Isaiah 41:21–43:28)

The Lord Presents His Servant

The Lord's comfort will come ultimately through the seed of Israel—the promised king to come in the line of David—as we have seen in Isaiah's first 39 chapters. In chapters 40–55, Isaiah shows the way the king will come: as a *servant*. Chapter 42 brings us the first of the "Servant Songs," unfolding further the beauty of God's sovereign redemptive plan. First, we are vividly reminded of how desperately this servant is needed.

DAY ONE—BEHOLD! (ISAIAH 41:21–42:4)

1. Isaiah here addresses one main reason God ordained the exile as punishment. Create a title and a brief outline for Isaiah 41:21–24.

2. In Isaiah 41:25–29, God sets forth his case and brings his proofs, with another reference to Cyrus—whose empire stretched far and wide. What is God's main point? What words and phrases stand out?

3. Note the third "Behold" (Isa. 42:1), which turns us from empty "nothing" to the huge reality of the promised one to come. Read Isaiah 42:1–4 slowly and carefully, writing down your initial observations of this first beautiful Servant Song.

4. Consider this figure to whom the Lord is pointing.

    a.   In the first three lines of Isaiah 42:1, what can we discern about his identity?

    b.   The servant here appears as an individual. How was this name applied differently in Isaiah 41:8–10?

    c.   What do we learn in Matthew 12:15–21?

5. The central mission of the servant comes in the repeated word *justice*. Observe all you can about the servant's mission of justice, in Isaiah 42:1–4. Then look at Isaiah 1:24–28 and 9:1–7 to recall and further observe this important theme of Isaiah.

6. In what ways does Isaiah 42:1–4 vividly communicate the manner in which this servant will accomplish justice? What pictures or details stand out?

7.   What questions might be left after this first Servant Song?

Day Two—Responding to the Servant (Isaiah 42:5–25)

1. God himself responds to this first portrait of the servant, looking at him and speaking directly to him, for all to hear.

   a.   Examine the parallel lines of poetry in Isaiah 42:5. What do they communicate, and how? Why does he begin this way?

LESSON 14 (ISAIAH 41:21–43:28)

b. God's covenant (v. 6) refers to God's unfailing promises to his people, from Adam to Noah, Abraham, Isaac, Jacob, David, and on and on to the one, finally, in whom all God's promises are fulfilled. Using his covenant name (LORD or *Yahweh*), what truths does God reveal about his covenant plan in Isaiah 42:6–8?

c. With one more "Behold," how does Isaiah 42:9 both tie up this whole section and lead to the next (see Isa. 42:10)?

2. In Isaiah 42:10–12, from where does the response come, and what is the tone and substance of it?

3. In Isaiah 42:13–17, the Lord describes the results of his justice. What do the details and pictures of these verses reveal about the Lord and the justice he brings?

4. The chapter ends with a sad summary of the response of God's people in Isaiah's time, a response that led to the exile described here. How does Isaiah 42:18–25 communicate both the people's nature and God's nature? What phrases stand out, and why? *Note: God's people are again called his "servant." Consider the telling contrast between the disobedient ones chosen to be God's servant, and the one servant who obeyed him perfectly. The one who came from their seed did for them what they could not do for themselves.*

5. Look back to Isaiah's commission in Isaiah 6:8–13. What strikes you, in relation to the verses we have just read (Isa. 42:18–25)?

DAY THREE—FEAR NOT, FOR I HAVE REDEEMED YOU (ISAIAH 43:1–13)

1. After the desolate end of chapter 42, the "But now" of Isaiah 43:1 breaks in with huge comfort. According to Isaiah 43:1 and 43:5–7 (bookends to this little section), what truths can we learn about the identity of those who belong to God, pictured here as called back out of exile (and ultimately called from earth's far corners, when Jesus comes again)?

2. Read and reread the two sets of parallel lines that make up the marvelous promises God gives to his people in Isaiah 43:2. What do these pictures make you see and understand?

3. These verses recall the exodus, in which God destroyed Egypt in order to redeem his people. In Isaiah 43:3–4, what truths can we find to explain such an exchange? *Note: Pause to wonder that God should stop, in his revelation, to say, "I love you."*

4. Isaiah 43:8–13 calls two groups of witnesses to God's declarations.

    a. Who makes up the group in verses 8–9? What is God's method and point in regard to them?

b. What is the identity of the second group (vv. 10–13)? What is God's method and point in regard to them? What words and phrases stand out?

5. Look back through Isaiah 43:1–13, in which God bares his heart to his people. What part(s) of these verses do you most need to hear today, and why?

Day Four—I Send to Babylon
(Isaiah 43:14–28)

1. In the next section, God's redemption is pictured everywhere we look! First, recall Isaiah 39:7, in which the Babylonian captivity was predicted. Then read Isaiah 43:14–15. What are the sources of comfort here, for God's people?

2. Isaiah 43:16–21 turns on the pivot of verses 18–19, which point back to the "former" exodus and ahead to the "new thing": the release from Babylon. How are the two things contrasted? What's the main point?

3. How amazing and sorrowful to read the verses following such glorious promises. This familiar rhythm in Isaiah increasingly reveals God's promised redemption and the people's utter inability to accomplish it for themselves. What repeated words set the tone in Isaiah 43:22–24? What is God's charge here?

4. From God's heavy charges, to the breaking forth of his amazing declaration in Isaiah 43:25, to the immediate cloud of the courtroom argument in Isaiah 43:26–28, the text establishes a tension without clearly resolving it at this point. How does Isaiah 43:25 stand out, especially in the context of this chapter, and how does it lead us to recall Isaiah 1?

5. How does Isaiah 43:26–28 present God's response to sin? How good or bad are we today at grasping this truth, and why? How can we better grasp it? *Note: "First father" may refer to Jacob, the father of Israel's twelve tribes—or perhaps Abraham—or even Adam . . . but, in any case, consider the part played by various kinds of leaders in encouraging sin among God's people.*

Day Five—Conclusions

1. What an amazing picture, in these chapters, of a God who so loves his people but who justly punishes their sin. How rich God's promise of a servant who will faithfully bring forth justice. Look back through Isaiah 41:21–43:28, focusing on the person of God—what we learn of him, his attributes, and his way of dealing with human beings. Write down several aspects of God that stand out to you, and then write a personal response— which could be in the form of a prayer, or questions, or simply a few sentences responding to the Lord God

who from the beginning ordained all of history for his redemptive purposes.

2. Look once more through the section and choose a verse or a short passage to write out and commit to memory. Be ready to share with your group the ways in which you find the verse (or verses) challenging, helpful, beautiful, etc.

Notes for Lesson 14

Lesson 15 (Isaiah 44–45)
THE LORD WILL SAVE, AND NO OTHER

Directly following the declaration of utter destruction for disobedient "Jacob" and "Israel" at the end of chapter 43 comes an amazing "But now" at the beginning of chapter 44.

DAY ONE—BUT NOW HEAR AND DO NOT FEAR (ISAIAH 44:1–8)

1. From Isaiah 44:1–2, analyze the relationship of God with his people. *Note: "Jeshurun" is an affectionate sort of nickname for Israel here.*

2. Isaiah 44:3–5 explains why we should not fear, as God's chosen people. What is the central picture at work through these verses, and what do the parts of the picture communicate?

3. From Isaiah 11:1–2; 32:14–16; 44:3–5, what observations can we make concerning the Holy Spirit, the third person of "God in three persons, blessed Trinity"?

4. Trace the names "Jacob" and "Israel" from Isaiah 43:28 through 44:5. What fear is given what wonderful answer through the course of these verses?

5. How can Isaiah 44:1–5 encourage us now, as God's people? Who comes to mind who might need to know this encouragement today?

6. How does Isaiah 44:6–8 provide a rock-solid foundation for the promises of verses 1–5? What aspects of God here help build this foundation?

DAY TWO—ONLY THE LORD HAS DONE IT (ISAIAH 44:9–23)

1. Read Isaiah 44:9–20. How do these verses follow logically the ones preceding them?

2. What is the central claim of this section (Isa. 44:9–20)? How would you summarize its argument?

3. How and where do we see even today the sad results of idolatry described in Isaiah 44:18–20?

4. The one living God, in contrast with all those idols, speaks and offers two commands that encase Isaiah 44:21–22.

    a.   What are these two commands, and why are they so crucial for God's people, including us?

    b.   With what truths (present, past, and future) does God support his commands?

Consider: The sovereign Lord of history looks into the future and counts it as certain as the past. We have seen and will see more examples of God's considering his redemptive plan so perfectly ordained as to be <u>done</u>, centuries before the coming of Christ our Redeemer.

5. Isaiah 44:23 responds! If you were to give a short devotional on this verse, what would be your outline? What would be your "take-away"?

DAY THREE—CYRUS, GOD'S ANOINTED?
(ISAIAH 44:24–45:13)

1. The redemption stated in Isaiah 44:23 is now expounded by the Redeemer. Isaiah 44:24–28 offers a string of "who" phrases culminating in the prediction concerning Cyrus—the Persian ruler who in 539 B.C. conquered the Babylonians and released the Jews from captivity to return home to rebuild their land of Judah, particularly their capital of Jerusalem. What does

each of these "who" phrases have to do with God's redemption of his people?

2. Cyrus becomes a picture of the greater deliverer to come. If God planned that greater deliverer and knew his name, then it is not so surprising that he planned this human deliverer and called him by name well over a century before Cyrus appeared on the stage of history. Read Isaiah 44:28–45:7.

a. In 44:28–45:3b, how is the great conqueror Cyrus portrayed, in relation to the Lord God? What words and phrases stand out to you? *Note: "Messiah" is a trans-literation of the Hebrew for "anointed one"—which translates into the Greek "Christos" or "Christ." To anoint (usually with oil) was to set something or someone apart as holy or kingly.*

LESSON 15 (ISAIAH 44–45)

b. In 45:3c–45:7, what is the point? What words and phrases stand out to you?

c. Stop to ponder God's huge revelations about himself in these verses. How do you respond? How does the world around us respond?

3. Isaiah 45:8 responds! What does the picture in this verse communicate? Compare this picture with that of Isaiah 44:3–4.

4. Isaiah 45:9–13 anticipates a different response to such an unlikely deliverer. God's people had been promised a king in the line of David; how should they welcome restoration under a pagan conqueror? How do the pictures of Isaiah 45:9–10 help communicate the message of verses 11–13 (in which "him" refers to Cyrus)?

5. How do these pictures help in dealing with God's sometimes incomprehensible plans? In what specific situations might these verses challenge and instruct you?

DAY FOUR—ALL THE ENDS OF THE
EARTH (ISAIAH 45:14–25)

1. No unbelieving king will prevail, finally. Look back
   through the following verses to recall Isaiah's vision
   of where history is heading: Isaiah 2:2–4; 9:1; 11:1–10.
   How does Isaiah 45:14 fit in?

2. In what ways, according to the previous verses, does
   the first line of Isaiah 45:15 appear true? How does
   Isaiah 45:15b–17 qualify and help process that apparent truth?

3. In what ways does Isaiah 45:18–19 (and this whole book!) answer the charge that God hides himself? According to these words, why can we trust what God is telling us in this book?

4. In Isaiah 45:20–21, God's call is not hidden, but goes out to all the nations with what argument? How do the terms in which God describes himself provide all the argument needed?

5. What a gracious command, and what a glorious vision in the final verses of this chapter! Read and reread Isaiah 45:22–25.

   a. Examine and comment on these verses' use of "every" and "all." How is the truth here both amazingly inclusive and soberingly exclusive?

   b. According to these verses, what aspects or qualities of God guarantee the truth of this vision?

   c. Why *righteousness* twice here? Why *righteousness* twice in Isaiah 45:8, where it rains down and bears fruit? (Look back to Isa. 1:26–27.) How is the Lord's righ-

teousness key to accomplishing the final promise of
Isaiah 45:25?

d. Yes, we must turn to the New Testament. Isaiah 45:23
    is referenced in Romans 14:11, and it appears most
    beautifully in Philippians 2:5–11. What strikes you,
    reading these New Testament verses?

DAY FIVE—CONCLUSIONS

1. How graciously and openly God has revealed himself and
    his redemptive purposes! His sovereign plan for Cyrus is
    impressive, but how much more impressive are his eternal
    plans for all the nations from which he will make a people
    for himself forever. Look back through Isaiah 44 and 45,
    focusing on God's revelation of himself, his attributes,
    and his way of dealing with human beings. Write down

several aspects of God that stand out to you, and then write a personal response—which could be in the form of a prayer, or questions, or simply a few sentences responding to the Lord God besides whom there is none.

2. Look once more through these chapters and choose a verse or a short passage to write out and commit to memory. Be ready to share with your group the ways in which you find the verse (or verses) challenging, helpful, beautiful, etc.

Notes for Lesson 15

Lesson 16 (Isaiah 46–48)

THE LORD'S PLANS
FOR CYRUS

The Lord continues to lay out his plans for Cyrus: to bring down Babylon, and to bring out God's people from Babylonian captivity. God reveals himself consistently and increasingly not only as the one who sets the course of history, but also as the one who hates and punishes sin—the sin of the idol-worshiping Babylonians *and* the sin of his disobedient people. The liberator Cyrus makes us long for a liberator who will not only release God's people from captivity but redeem God's people from sin.

DAY ONE—GOD HAS PURPOSED;
GOD WILL DO IT (ISAIAH 46)

1. Compare and contrast the picture of the Babylonian false gods Bel and Nebo (Isa. 46:1–2) with the picture of the true God (Isa. 46:3–4). What contemporary version of these comparisons might one make today?

2. In Isaiah 46:5–7, what's the main point? What aspects of idol worship are highlighted here?

3. In Isaiah 46:8–11, God calls his people to remember how his word has been accomplished in the past (recall his prophecies regarding Assyria and other nations in the first part of the book), and to trust that his word now declared to them (particularly regarding Cyrus, as in v. 11) will be accomplished in the future. What aspects of God emerge strongly in these verses? What phrases stand out?

4. How does God reveal his knowledge of those to whom he speaks, in Isaiah 46:8–12? (Recall Isa. 1:4.)

5. Examine the solution to this dilemma as God states it in Isaiah 46:13. The previous chapter also closed with the solution (Isa. 45:24–25). What similarities do you find— and what further unfolding of the solution? (Among other things, don't forget to notice the promise of glory that ends both chapters; learn all you can from these verses about the glory promised for us, his people.)

DAY TWO—BABYLON WILL BE PUNISHED (ISAIAH 47)

1. In Isaiah 47:1–4, Babylon is pictured as a pampered princess. What do the images here imply concerning the nature of her downfall to come (at the hand of Cyrus)? How do the three names of God in verse 4 offer an explanation for her punishment?

2. How does Isaiah 47:5–7 expose the wrong thinking of the Babylonians who would conquer God's people and take them into exile?

3. In Isaiah 47:8–11, what characteristics of the Babylonians emerge, and how will these characteristics be dealt with? What words and phrases are especially revealing?

4. Isaiah 47:12–15 delves into the evils of the "sorceries" and "enchantments" introduced in verse 9. With what tone and through what sorts of arguments are these evils condemned here?

5. Look again through Isaiah 47, which condemns the evils and proclaims the penalty of people who do not acknowledge the one true God. What implications and applications can we find for our world today?

Day Three—A Call to Israel (Isaiah 48:1–11)

1. The Lord now addresses his people, who will eventually be redeemed from captivity. According to Isaiah 48:1–2, list the things these people would cite as evidence of their identity as God's people. What problem here, however, sours it all? What parallel or similar situations come to mind?

LESSON 16 (ISAIAH 46–48)

2. God again speaks of former and new things, the
   former things being those the people have heard
   prophesied and then seen accomplished. In Isaiah
   48:3–8, how does God explain his reasoning behind
   these pronouncements? What view of human nature
   is God revealing here?

3. Isaiah 48:9–11 reveals God's primary concern as he deals
   with his rebellious people.

   a. How is this primary concern effectively communicated?

b. How can these words and phrases challenge *our* concerns and motivations?

c. What is it that God does for his own sake, according to these verses? How will this bring glory to his name?

4. How have you perhaps known or witnessed the furnace of affliction to refine a child of God and bring glory to his name?

DAY FOUR—LISTEN! (ISAIAH 48:12–22)

1. Examine the two calls to listen, in Isaiah 48:12–13 and Isaiah 48:14–15. What is the nature of each call, and what is the logical relationship between the two?

2. The one who answers God's call seems to emerge gradually, starting in Isaiah 48:16 and stepping forth again as the revealed servant figure in the next chapter. What clues do you find to the identity of the speaker in Isaiah 48:16? (Recall Isa. 11:1–2; 42:1.)

3. The Lord God who sends this servant (Isa. 48:16) is the Lord God who is related in what ways to his people, according to Isaiah 48:17?

4. How does Isaiah 48:18–19 evidence God's redeeming love *and* the people's desperate need for a Redeemer? (Recall Genesis 12:1–2; 22:15–18.)

5. Isaiah 48:20–21 continues to affirm God's redemption. As the rescue from Babylon is celebrated, how is *another, earlier rescue* recalled—with what details? With what questions and tensions are we left here?

6. What is that final verse of Isaiah 48 doing there? How does it appropriately, if suddenly, end the chapter (and prepare the way for the second Servant Song, in the next chapter)?

DAY FIVE—CONCLUSIONS

1. How amazing it must have been for the prophet Isaiah to peer into the mysteries of redemptive history as this vision was revealed to him! How amazing it is, even for us, to witness the merciful plan of God for sinful people, through a Redeemer who indeed brought his righteousness and his salvation near to us (Isa. 26:13). Look back through Isaiah 46–48, focusing on this God who revealed himself so clearly through this faithful prophet. What do we learn of the Lord God, his attributes, and his way of dealing with human beings? Write down several aspects of God that stand out to you, and then write your own response—which could be in the form of a prayer, or questions, or simply a few sentences that express your personal response.

2. Look once more through the section and choose a verse or a short passage to write out and commit to memory. Be ready to share with your group the ways in which you find the verse (or verses) challenging, helpful, beautiful, etc.

Notes for Lesson 16

Lesson 17 (Isaiah 49–50)

THE LORD'S SERVANT SPEAKS

We're entering the heart of these chapters about the servant, encountering here the second and third Servant Songs. As this servant steps forward and speaks, he comes more and more into focus before our eyes, as the one who took on himself the form of a servant in order to accomplish faithfully God's redemptive purposes for all nations of the earth.

DAY ONE—LISTEN TO THE SERVANT (ISAIAH 49:1–6)

1. Look back to Isaiah 48 to clarify the inadequacy of the *people of Israel* to act the part of God's chosen *servant*, even though he has called them by that name. Read the second Servant Song (Isa. 49:1–6) to hear from the one servant God appoints in their place. How does Isaiah 49:5 clarify God's calling of this servant?

2. Observe all you can, in the servant's testimony of Isaiah 49:1c–3, about God's calling and equipping him. After you have observed the passage, consider how the following verses deepen and confirm its meaning: Isaiah 7:10–14; 9:6; Ephesians 6:17; Hebrews 4:12; Revelation 1:12–16.

3. Considering the people this servant is called to replace and redeem (and perhaps anticipating the "deeply despised, abhorred" of v. 7), why might his lament in Isaiah 49:4 be justified? However, how does he answer his own lament?

4. The mission of this servant is expressed in two parts, in
   Isaiah 49:5–6.

   a. Whose words are these, and who is speaking? What
      is the effect?

   b. What is the first stated and then the second stated
      but ultimate mission here? (Recall also the chapter's
      first two lines.)

5. How do the following verses shed light on the servant's
   ultimate mission: Genesis 12:3; Isaiah 2:1–4; Matthew
   28:16–20?

DAY TWO—THUS SAYS THE LORD (ISAIAH 49:7–14)

1. Like the first Servant Song, the second is followed by the Lord's own commentary. Read Isaiah 49:7–13, and then look back to Isaiah 42:5–13. What similarities do you notice?

2. In Isaiah 49:7, how are the names and identity of the Lord key to the amazing promise he offers? How do the identity and description of the one to whom he speaks make the promise even more amazing?

3. As the Lord continues to address his servant, how does Isaiah 49:8–10 connect the servant with pictures of the return from Babylonian exile?

4. How does Isaiah 49:8–10 grow, through verses 11–13, into an even larger understanding of "salvation" and "covenant"? *Note: Recall that highway of holiness back in Isaiah 35:8–10 and the one in Isaiah 40:3–5.*

5. In Isaiah 49:14, God's people, perhaps pictured here still in exile, speak up. What is the effect of this verse, in the flow of the passage? How might this verse instruct us now?

DAY THREE—THUS SAYS THE LORD, CONT'D (ISAIAH 49:15–50:3)

1. As God answers Zion's "But," how do his pictures communicate the nature of his love for his people (Isa. 49:15–16)? Which picture would you especially choose to set in your mind through this day, and why?

2. Read Isaiah 49:17–26, where the Lord's words to his exiled people continue. *What* will the Lord do for his people? *How* will he do it? *For what purpose* will he do it?

3. Who are all these offspring of Zion promised here? When the Jewish people returned to their land after being liberated by Cyrus, they did not grow into a large nation that overflowed their land. Look back to Isaiah 11:10–12; look ahead to Isaiah 54:1–3; look far ahead to Galatians 3:7–9.

4. In Isaiah 50, God begins by clarifying his right and power to punish or deliver. He had not divorced his people (again pictured here as a woman), which would involve a binding certificate; nor had he sold her into slavery, as one in debt who is obliged to give a family member to pay for that debt. How does God explain his reason for the exile (Isa. 50:1–2)?

5. What aspects of God does Isaiah 50:2–3 mean to show? What pictures help us see?

DAY FOUR—THE THIRD SERVANT SONG (ISAIAH 50:4–11)

1. There is one man (recall Isa. 50:2a) to answer God's call, and he steps up to speak in verse 4. As you read the servant's words in Isaiah 50:4–9, trace and comment on his references to the "Lord GOD"—sometimes translated Sovereign LORD.

2. In Isaiah 50:4–9, observe all you can, specifically about the servant's ability to *speak* and to *hear*. What resulting character traits grow from such abilities, according to these verses?

3. Read Matthew 27:27–31; Mark 1:35–39; I Peter 2:18–25. How might these verses help illuminate Isaiah 50:4–9?

4. How would you summarize the ways in which this servant offers an example to God's people?

5. Isaiah 50:10–11 follows the servant's words again with a kind of commentary and with a theme of *light*. Examine and contrast the two very different responses addressed through this theme.

DAY FIVE—CONCLUSIONS

1. What a Lord God, who can compare himself to the mother of a nursing child and who can rebuke the oceans. This is the God who sends his Servant to suffer and to pay for the iniquities of a sinful people. Look back through Isaiah 49–50, focusing on the Lord God, and asking what we learn of him, his attributes, and his way of dealing with human beings. Write down several aspects of God that stand out to you, and then write your personal response, which could be in the form of a prayer, or questions, or simply a few sentences that express your listening response to the Lord God who speaks to us through these inspired words.

2. Look once more through the section and choose a verse or a short passage to write out and commit to memory. Be ready to share with your group the ways in which you find the verse (or verses) challenging, helpful, beautiful, etc.

Notes for Lesson 17

Lesson 18 (Isaiah 51–53)

THE LORD'S PLANS
FOR HIS SERVANT

DAY ONE—LISTEN TO ME! (ISAIAH 51:1–8)

1. Find the three calls to listen in Isaiah 51:1–8. To whom are these calls addressed? How has Isaiah 50 prepared us for these calls?

2. In Isaiah 51:1–3, what's the point and what's the comfort? How do these verses recall the promises of Isaiah 49:17–23?

3. What is the focus of the hope in Isaiah 51:4–6? Recall also Isaiah 46:12–13.

4. How do both Isaiah 51:6 and 51:7–8 (*and* Isa. 50:9) adjust our perspectives on what will last and what will not? What commands accompany these perspective adjustments, and why? (See also 2 Peter 3:10–13.)

5. Spend a few more minutes answering the call to *listen* to the truths spoken by the Lord to his people in this section, especially those in question 4. How do you respond? What are the implications of these truths for you, personally and practically?

Day Two—Awake, Awake! (Isaiah 51:9–23)

1. Isaiah 51:9–11 responds enthusiastically to the Lord's words! What is the point, and how do the allusions to past events contribute to the point? (See Isa. 30:7, where Rahab is a mocking nickname for Egypt, perhaps with an allusion to a Canaanite mythical monster. See also Isa. 35:8–10.)

2. God speaks again, in Isaiah 51:12–16, and he is certainly not asleep. How does God identify and characterize both himself and the "*you*" to whom he speaks? Note the "I am" phrases enclosing this passage.

3. Who is the one called to awaken in Isaiah 51:17–20, and what does the picture communicate? (See Ps. 75:7–8; Jer. 25:15–18.) What other vivid picture is used in this passage, and how?

4. After such torment, what hope we find in the promises of Isaiah 51:21–23! How does that central picture from the previous verses develop here, to explain what God will do?

5. Look ahead to Isaiah 52:1–2. What is the effect of encountering this new call right after the last verses of chapter 51?

Day Three—Good News! (Isaiah 52:1–12)

1. Look again at Isaiah 52:1–2. How does the picture of God's people as a woman develop here? (Recall Isa. 1:21. Consider also Rev. 19:6–8; 21:1–2, 22–27.)

2. According to Isaiah 52:3–6, with what is God concerned in all kinds of captivity and redemption? (Think back to the exodus story, referenced in these verses. Consider Ex. 3:13–15.)

3. Isaiah 52:7–8 pictures joyful proclamation of the good news—the redemption of God's people. What do you observe about the substance of this good news? What light does the apostle Paul shed on this joyful proclamation in Romans 10:13–15?

4. Isaiah 52:9–12 uses several starting points from Israel's history to reach out toward the full meaning of this redemption.

   a. Verses 9–10 begin with a celebration of the exiles' return to Jerusalem; how do these verses "reach out" to celebrate even more than that?

b. Verse 11 perhaps pictures the priests receiving back
from Cyrus the temple vessels that the Babylonians
had carried off, and bearing them back to Jerusalem
(Ezra 1). How does the picture of God's people as
consecrated priests grow as redemption unfolds?
(See 2 Cor. 6:14–7:1; 1 Peter 2:4–5, 9.)

c. How does verse 12 move from a particular point in
history to a promise for all God's people? (See Ex.
12:11; 13:21–22; 14:19–20.)

DAY FOUR—THE FOURTH AND LAST
SERVANT SONG (ISAIAH 52:13–53:12)

All the ends of the earth shall see the salvation of our God!
How will such promises ever be fulfilled? In this context we arrive
at the fourth Servant Song, as the servant's redemptive work is
revealed more fully than ever before. The whole prophecy of

LESSON 18 (ISAIAH 51–53)

Isaiah, from chapter 1, has made us long for this revelation of just how the sin of those God calls his own would be dealt with, according to his righteousness and justice! Read through the whole song, aloud if possible, aiming to get a sense of its whole shape—enclosed by verses of victory and with the servant's death for our sins at the center.

1. Consider the song's introductory section (Isa. 52:13–15).

   a. What aspects of the servant's life are foretold here?

   b. Find this word "sprinkle" in Leviticus 4:1–6 and Hebrews 9:19–22. What does it mean that this servant will *sprinkle* the nations?

   c. According to Romans 15:20–21, how did Paul see himself helping to fulfill this prophecy concerning the nations?

2. Consider Isaiah 53:1–3.

   a. Meditate on the descriptive phrases. What kind of portrait emerges here? What details and pictures stand out?

   b. Look ahead to the apostle Paul, who evidently knew and loved this book. How is Isaiah 53:1 part of the logic of Paul's argument in Romans 10:14–17? (How does John 12:37–40 shed further light?)

   c. Read Isaiah 52:10 with 53:1–2. What do you observe about this "arm of the LORD"?

3. Isaiah 53:4–6 presents the heart of the song and the heart of the servant's mission.

    a.   What words in verses 4–6 explain what of *ours* this servant took on himself? How do these words together communicate the depths of his suffering for us?

    b.   In what ways do these verses communicate the purposeful nature of the servant's suffering?

    c.   How do the two words describing the *results* often get redefined by the world? What does each word mean, according to this context? (See also 1 Peter 2:24–25.)

4. How does the picture of the sheep develop from verse 6 to verse 7? In Isaiah 53:7–8, how do we see presented both an apparent victim and yet a purposeful sufferer?

5. What is the important truth about this servant in Isaiah 53:9? (How might this verse connect with Matt. 27:57–60?)

6. How do Acts 8:26–35 and 1 Peter 2:21–23 present the identity of the servant described in Isaiah 53:7–9?

7. In what ways does Isaiah 53:10–12 clarify God's ultimate purposes at work in his servant's suffering? (See also Acts 2:23; Gal. 3:29; 1 Peter 1:3–4, 10–11.)

Day Five—Conclusions

1. We have moved this week into the very heart of the servant and the heart of God's eternal redemptive purposes. How amazing to think of Isaiah writing these truths centuries before the promised servant came to earth. Look back through Isaiah 51–53, considering what these chapters reveal about the Lord God, his attributes, and his way of dealing with human beings. Write down several aspects of God that stand out to you, and then write your personal response—which could be in the form of a prayer, or questions, or simply a few sentences responding to this sovereign, redeeming God.

2. Look once more through the section and choose a verse or a short passage to write out and commit to memory. Be ready to share with your group the ways in which you find the verse (or verses) challenging, helpful, beautiful, etc.

Notes for Lesson 18

Lesson 19 (Isaiah 54–55)

THE LORD CALLS OUT TO US

Isaiah's middle "Servant Section" ends with a call to respond, a call providing a finale both for the fourth Servant Song and for this whole remarkable tapestry of Isaiah 40–55. We have peered with Isaiah into the Babylonian captivity and release—and, through that prophetic lens, into God's larger plan to redeem his people from an even greater captivity. These chapters have revealed God's plan of salvation through his beloved Servant. Now, as we continue to peer into this salvation, we are called to respond!

DAY ONE—SING! (ISAIAH 54:1–10)

1. We know this picture in Isaiah 54:1–3! What does it communicate here? How do these verses develop themes we have seen consistently in Isaiah?

2. This redemption of God's people from all nations, through his Servant, demands a response.

    a. Consider the commands in Isaiah 54:1. Do you know this response? How might we know it better?

    b. What response is called for in Isaiah 54:2? What is, or should be, involved in this response?

3. What response is called for in Isaiah 54:4, as the picture of God's people as a woman continues? What aspects of God in Isaiah 54:4–5 make all this possible? *Consider: How are these verses so needed and crucial for every believer?*

4. How does Isaiah 54:6–8 *continue* to develop this picture, with even another variation? Through careful observation of these verses, what can you learn about God?

5. In Isaiah 54:9–10, examine the parallel with the days of Noah, to observe in what ways God consistently deals with his people. (See also Gen. 9:8–17.) What words stand out, and why?

DAY TWO—LOOK AT THIS CITY (ISAIAH 54:11–17)

1. The picture of God's people shifts here from a woman to a city—which should not surprise us! Stop to sum up briefly how Isaiah has used the picture of the city. (For example, you might recall Isa. 1:26–27; 4:2–6; chapters 24–26.)

2. What details of the picture in Isaiah 54:11–12 stand out? What can we discern about the speaker here, and about the one he addresses?

3. Comment on Isaiah 54:11–12 in relation to Isaiah 26:1–4 and Revelation 21:1–14.

4. How might the parallel lines of Isaiah 54:13 work together, in this description of the city's children (the "offspring" we have seen promised, for example in Isa. 53:10)?

5. What a picture of security in Isaiah 54:14–17! Consider how this security is established, and how and to whom it is given.

6. Look back through Isaiah 54:11–17. We are still today heading for the perfect final city, but in what ways do these verses celebrate the place where we live as God's people now, in Christ, that Servant from whom all the offspring come?

Day Three—Come! (Isaiah 55:1–7)

1. Repeatedly we have seen the promises to Israel stretch out to all nations. This last chapter of Isaiah's middle section continues the pattern, reaching out with its call to . . . *whom*? What qualifications do you find in Isaiah 55:1? What do these pictures tell us about the ones called?

2. How is the picture of eating and drinking developed in Isaiah 55:1–2? What kinds of food/drink are mentioned, and why? What's the point, and how does it apply to us?

3. How does Isaiah 55:3–7 expand the point made in verse 2? What is the effect of these commands to listen? Can you sum up what God wants us to hear?

4. Let us remember the biblical context for God's *everlasting covenant*, his *steadfast, sure love for David (Isa. 55:3)*.

a. Summarize the way Psalm 89:20–37 expresses God's steadfast, covenant love for David.

b. In Isaiah 9:6–7, how is the promised child the fulfillment of all these promises?

5. How amazing that all these promises, fulfilled in Jesus Christ, come through him to us—and to all the nations. What a call to come and eat! Learn everything you can about this call, as it continues in Isaiah 55:6–7: its accompanying commands, its timing, its audience, the nature of its rewards. . . .

Day Four—Finishing with the "For's" (Isaiah 55:8–13)

1. This concluding call of the middle chapters ends with four "For's"—four huge, conclusive reasons why we should answer this call. How does Isaiah 55:7 lead logically into the first "For" of Isaiah 55:8?

2. How do the two "For's" (in Isaiah 55:8–9) work together to make one point? Why is this point so crucial for us to understand?

3. Another "For" begins Isaiah 55:10–11. What is the logical link into these powerful verses about God's word? How does the *picture* work here, communicating what truths about the word of God? *Consider: What do these verses tell us about the call of this chapter? What do these verses tell us about the servant whose mouth God made like a sharp sword? Look back*

271

to 40:6—8 to see how this whole section is framed with affirmations concerning the word of God.

4. We've twice received a *humbling* "For" (Isa. 55:8—9), reminding us why we needed to heed the call. We've had a *faith-inspiring* "For" (Isa. 55:10—11), reminding us how deeply we could trust the call. How would you characterize the "For" of Isaiah 55:12—13? How are these verses appropriate to end this middle section of Isaiah?

5. To what has release from exile pointed, consistently, throughout this section of Isaiah? (See Isa. 40:1–2.) How is the response of Isaiah 55:12–13 appropriate for such a deliverance?

6. Finally, focus on the *pictures* in these final verses. How do they awaken all our senses and emotions? How do they portray not only our present but also our future joy?

DAY FIVE—CONCLUSIONS

1. What a joyous, universe-wide call ends this "Servant section" of Isaiah! Such a call reminds us that we are not just taking in truth here; we are hearing God speak, and his word demands a response. Take a moment to look back through Isaiah 54–55, focusing on the person of God—what we

learn of him, his attributes, and his way of dealing with human beings. Write down several aspects of God that stand out to you, and then write a personal response—which could be in the form of a prayer, or questions, or simply a few sentences responding to the Lord God who through his perfect servant made a way for his people to find the ultimate redemption from the ultimate exile.

2. Look once more through the section and choose a verse or a short passage to write out and commit to memory. Be ready to share with your group the ways in which you find the verse (or verses) challenging, helpful, beautiful, etc.

Notes for Lesson 19

Lesson 20 (Isaiah 56–58)

THE LORD'S PLANS
FOR HIS PEOPLE

Let's remember where we are—at a rather exciting point in Isaiah. The first section of the book (Isaiah 1–39) addressed God's pre-exilic people, warning them concerning sin, the results of sin, and the need for repentance and trust in the king of heaven—*and* promising that king's ultimate perfect rule. The book's second section (Isaiah 40–55) looked ahead to God's people in exile, promising comfort and a release pointing ahead to an ultimate release from sin, through God's own Servant. Chapter 56 begins the book's third and final section (Isaiah 56–66), in which the prophet looks ahead to God's people returned from exile. We were given the plan of a renewed Jerusalem from the book's first chapter; we saw in the book's middle section the means for this renewal; we focus in the end on the hope of this renewal. It is a hope for an eternal city, and for the final conqueror who will bring an end to all sin.

DAY ONE—HOW TO LIVE NOW (ISAIAH 56:1–8)

1. Look through Isaiah 56. Then consider Isaiah 56:1 in light of the middle chapters it follows. How do these words have more meaning because of what has come before?

2. One clear means of "doing righteousness" involves keeping the Sabbath.

   a. In Isaiah 56:2, 4, 6, what aspects of the Sabbath stand out as important?

   b. According to Exodus 31:12–17, why is the Sabbath important for those belonging to the Lord?

c. For believers in Jesus Christ, to what kind of rest from work does the Sabbath ultimately point? (Refer to Heb. 4:1–10, not to explain all the difficulties but to glean the main point.)

3. Consider the large scope of Isaiah 56:1–8.

a. What sorts of people are called to "hold fast my covenant" (that is, hear and follow his revealed Word)?

b. In what ways might we call God's promises to these people large in scope?

c. What light is shed on this passage by John 10:14–16, and, in reference to the eunuch, Deuteronomy 23:1 and Acts 8:26–38?

4. How is the *place* important, in Isaiah 56:5–8? Before answering, briefly look through 2 Chronicles 7:1–3; Mark 11:15–19; John 2:13–21; Revelation 21:1–2, 22–26. Then write one sentence summing up the significance of this place.

5. How are we seeing the reality of Isaiah 56:1–8 (and Isaiah 2:1–5) coming true even now? According to these verses, how can we play our part in seeing these promises come to fruition?

DAY TWO—JARRING REALITY
(ISAIAH 56:9–57:10)

1. In Isaiah 56:9–12, the promised ideal of God's worshiping, obedient people jars suddenly with the not-ideal reality.

   a. What's the picture, and what's the problem?

   b. What further light on this picture can you find in Isaiah 9:14–17; 28:7–8; 53:6; 55:4?

   c. What New Testament light shines on this picture, in 1 Peter 5:1–5?

2. The picture of a sinful people continues in Isaiah 57, with reference by contrast to the righteous ones in their midst. How is the death of the righteous portrayed from a variety of perspectives, in Isaiah 57:1–2? (See also Rev. 14:13.)

3. As the righteous pass quietly away, what is happening around them? Read the violent condemnation of Isaiah 57:3–10. Describe and react to the array of *attitudes* and *actions* among the ungodly here. (Recall Isaiah 1:21.)

4. These verses are dark. As you look back through this day of study, what strikes you as especially important for us to see and understand today, in our context?

DAY THREE—GOD WILL HEAL (ISAIAH 57:11–21)

1. Look back through Isaiah 57:1–10 to identify who is speaking and how you can tell. Then read on, in Isaiah 57:11–13, where this speaker emerges very personally. What are the main points of his condemnation of the idol worshipers?

2. That "But" in Isaiah 57:13 leads into a beautiful, compassionate conclusion to this chapter. In order for his people to "take refuge in him," for what does

God call in Isaiah 57:14? What does this picture mean? (Recall 40:1–5.)

3. What happens right in the midst of Isaiah 57:15? Observe everything you can about the two wonderful parts of this verse.

4. In Isaiah 57:16–17, what aspects of the people does God point out—and, in the process, what aspects of himself does God reveal?

5. The chapter ends with a huge contrast.

    a.   First, note all the things we can learn about the peace that is brought about in Isaiah 57:18–19.

    b.   Note all the things we can learn about the lack of peace in Isaiah 57:20–21. Be sure to note that graphic picture in verse 20.

    c.   Having read these verses (and recalling Isa. 26:2–3 and 53:5), how would you sum up Isaiah's conception of peace?

6. How have you experienced or witnessed this kind of peace and/or lack of peace?

DAY FOUR—FALSE AND TRUE DELIGHT (ISAIAH 58)

1. Read through Isaiah 58. What is happening in the first verse, and how can such a cry lead to hope rather than despair?

2. Fasting becomes the issue used to reveal the sins of "my people." How would you outline Isaiah 58:2–5? What application might be here for us today?

3. The rest of the chapter breaks into three cycles of a wonderful rhythm. First, find these three cycles of true obedience/resulting blessings in Isaiah 58:6–14. Then read carefully the three sections that state the true obedience God requires. What themes do you find? What kinds of obedience mark true people of faith?

4. Look back to Isaiah 1:12–17. What do you notice, in relation to Isaiah 58?

5. But now read the promises of God for his people, the "*Then* . . ." sections, the blessings he will pour out on us when we come with contrite obedience before him.

   a. In the picture of Isaiah 58:8–9b, what has happened to the sinful people, and how? What will characterize their lives now?

   b. In Isaiah 58:10c–12, the light breaks forth again. How are these pictures especially appropriate for a people who will return from a long exile? How are these pictures appropriate for *any* of God's needy people? Which picture(s) stands out to you, and why?

c. In what ways does Isaiah 58:14 bring wonderful closure to the whole chapter? How might you summarize the main point of chapter 58?

DAY FIVE—CONCLUSIONS

1. After glimpsing that servant so clearly in Isaiah's middle section, how amazing to dive back into the sinful

reality of those for whom he came to suffer and die. In light of God's merciful salvation, the sin appears even more dreadful and the hope more glorious. This will be the case through the end of the book. Look back through Isaiah 56–58, focusing on this God who has mercifully revealed himself in these pages. What do we learn of him, his attributes, and his way of dealing with human beings? Write down several aspects of God that stand out to you, and then write your own personal response—which could be in the form of a prayer, or questions, or simply a few sentences responding to the Lord God who, when we cry humbly to him, answers, "Here I am."

2. Look once more through the section and choose a verse or a short passage to write out and commit to memory.

Be ready to share with your group the ways in which you find the verse (or verses) challenging, helpful, beautiful, etc.

Notes for Lesson 20

Lesson 21 (Isaiah 59–60)

THE LORD LIGHTS UP
THE FUTURE

In chapter 59, Isaiah dives deep again into the people's iniquities, but then rises high into a vision of God's answer to those iniquities—an answer that grows, in Isaiah 60, into a magnificent glimpse of the eternal glory of God together with his people.

DAY ONE—INIQUITY, INIQUITY (ISAIAH 59:1–15B)

1. How does Isaiah 59:1–3 answer the questions in Isaiah 58:3? How do the pictures of hands, etc., communicate vividly the point of these verses?

2. After the problem is stated in Isaiah 59:1–3, it is dramatically elaborated in Isaiah 59:4–8.

    a.   What sorts of wrongs are charged in these verses? What repeated words and concepts emerge?

    b.   How do the pictures help communicate the nature of these wrongs?

    c.   How does verse 8 offer an appropriate conclusion to this section—and a version of a picture we recognize?

3. In Isaiah 59:9–15b, who is speaking, and how is this significant?

4. Examine the progression of ideas and pictures in Isaiah 59:9–11. What do you see?

5. Now examine the whole section, Isaiah 59:9–15b. What repeated words do you find from beginning to end? What is the effect of such repetition, and what is the main message here?

DAY TWO—THE LORD SAW . . .
(ISAIAH 59:15C–21)

1. Read Isaiah 59:15c–20, where God again is pictured in human terms, so that we can better grasp just what he has done. First, in Isaiah 59:15cd, what do we learn about God's relation to the iniquity just described?

2. Recall Isaiah 50:2–4 and 53:1–2. How do these verses connect with the man who is like God's own outstretched arm in Isaiah 59:16?

3. Isaiah 59:17–19 is like a story (a true one!). What part of the story does each verse unfold? What is the main point of this story?

4. God's work of salvation involves both his wrath and redemption from his wrath. What do you learn of this redemption, in Isaiah 59:20? How has this whole chapter made clear the only source of this redemption?

5. In Isaiah 59:21, God speaks, referring to *them* (those who "turn from transgression"), and then addressing *you*.

   a. To help identify this "you," read Isaiah 42:1, 6; 49:1–2; 53:10.

   b. How is God's promise here based on himself?

c. How can we as God's redeemed people receive this covenant promise personally? (See Titus 3:4–7.)

DAY THREE—ARISE, SHINE! (ISAIAH 60:1–14)

1. Following these glorious promises, Isaiah 60 looks forward to their glorious fulfillment. What's the picture here, and how does it develop in Isaiah 60:1–3?

2. How might you sum up what is happening in Isaiah 60:1–14? What details stand out?

3. Consider the role of God in these verses. What is he doing? What is he after? Refer to specific phrases.

4. How does Isaiah 2:1–5 help explain Isaiah 60:1–14?

5. What phrases call for or describe the response of God's people? Put some of these phrases in a prayer, a poem,

an outline . . . in some form that challenges you to show
forth this response more and more clearly.

DAY FOUR—YOUR GOD WILL BE YOUR GLORY (ISAIAH 60:15–22)

1. Isaiah continues to unfold the magnificent vision of
   what God has in store for his redeemed people. For
   each of the following pairs of verses, answer these
   three questions:

   - What is one main aspect of our future hope that
     these verses emphasize?

   - Explain how an image or picture in these verses helps
     communicate the point.

   - What aspects of God stand out in these verses?

a.   Isaiah 60:15–16

b.   Isaiah 60:17–18

c.   Isaiah 60:19–20

    d.   Isaiah 60:21–22

2. Much as we can see various aspects of these promises fulfilled now, through Jesus Christ and his Spirit among his people, we know the ultimate fulfillment will come in that New Jerusalem revealed even more fully to the apostle John. Look back through Isaiah 60, and then to Revelation 21. What common pictures and themes do you find?

3. Muse on these promises. Do you really believe them? If we took these promises more to heart, in what ways might that change the way we live now?

DAY FIVE—CONCLUSIONS

1. What a hope! What a sinful people! What a God who made such a hope possible for such a sinful people! This week's chapters have illuminated the depths of the sin and the heights of the hope. Look back through Isaiah 59–60, focusing on the God who brought light out of the darkness through *the man* who brought righteousness near to us. What do you learn of God, his attributes, and his way of dealing with human beings? Write down several aspects of God that stand out to you, and then write a personal response—which could be in the form of a prayer, or

questions, or simply a few sentences responding to the God of our salvation.

2. Look once more through the section and choose a verse or a short passage to write out and commit to memory. Be ready to share with your group the ways in which you find the verse (or verses) challenging, helpful, beautiful, etc.

Notes for Lesson 21

Lesson 22 (Isaiah 61:1–63:6)

The Lord Has Anointed Him

Day One—The Anointed One Speaks (Isaiah 61:1–9)

The final chapters bring to a climax all the promises and all the themes of the book. How remarkable to hear this messianic voice in chapter 61—now not focusing on a servant's suffering, but rather looking far ahead to the victory of redeeming and establishing a people of everlasting joy.

1. Read the first long sentence: Isaiah 61:1–3. What are your first impressions? How can we recognize this speaker, especially looking back to Isaiah 11:1–4; 42:1–4; 48:16.

2. What has the Lord anointed this one to do? List the seven infinitives (*to bring, to bind up* . . .) that describe his work (Isa. 61:1–3), and then observe and comment on this list.

3. How do the rich pictures in Isaiah 61:3 help communicate the nature of the transformation this anointed one will accomplish? What is the goal of this transformation? Connect this verse with the previous chapter's statement of the same goal.

4. In Luke 4:16–21, in what amazing way is the interpretation of this passage clarified? Why do you think Jesus stops where he does in quoting this passage?

5. About whom does Isaiah 61:4 continue to speak? How might this verse express comfort both for returned exiles and for many, many more—including us?

6. What blessings are promised to God's people in Isaiah 61:5–9? What in these verses assures us that all these promises are true?

DAY TWO—FOR ZION'S SAKE
(ISAIAH 61:10–62:7)

1. It is not clear who speaks in Isaiah 61:10–11. What do you think, and why? What do these vivid pictures communicate?

2. Some think Isaiah 62:1 brings again the voice of the Messiah; some think this is Isaiah's inspired voice. In any case, explain the motivation of such zeal to speak. In what ways might this zeal instruct and challenge us?

3. Isaiah 62:2–5 offers to God's people a glorious picture of what they will become, through the salvation

accomplished by the promised Messiah. In examining these verses, relish them as promises to be claimed now for those who have believed in the Christ who came— as well as promises to be fulfilled perfectly at Christ's second coming.

a. Follow the word "righteousness" from Isaiah 61:10 to 62:2. What characterizes this promised state? Why is this word so significant, in light of where we've come in this book?

b. Here again God's people are portrayed in terms of a woman. What beautiful details stand out? How does this passage connect to previous portrayals?

c.   Stop to notice God's role in these verses. What is he doing, and what details stand out?

4.   Isaiah 62:6–7 pictures watchmen set by the Lord (perhaps the Messiah continues speaking here) to serve until all these promises are wholly fulfilled. To whom are these words addressed? List the aspects of this watchman role; which aspects challenge you most personally?

Day Three—Clear the Way for the City (Isaiah 62:8–12)

1. The fulfillment of all these promises, however, does not depend on the watchmen's work. According to Isaiah 62:7–9, on what aspects of God can the watchmen depend?

2. Observe and comment on the scene of final fulfillment in Isaiah 62:7–9. What's going on, and where? What words might best characterize this scene?

3. In light of such a hope, what is our present role? List all the imperatives (commands!) in Isaiah 62:10–11. Examine these commands, the way they are offered, and the associated pictures. What do we learn here about what we are to be doing, as the people of God?

4. Examine the names for God's people in Isaiah 62:12 (note the two pairs of parallel lines). How has the book so far prepared us to understand the meaning of these names?

5. Look back through Isaiah 62. What is the main tone(s) of this chapter? How does this chapter affect your perspective on history—and on your role in it?

DAY FOUR—THE DAY OF VENGEANCE (ISAIAH 63:1–6)

1. For this first question, simply read and meditate. Read the drama with its amazing dialogue in Isaiah 63:1–6. Then reread Isaiah 59:15c–19; 61:2; and 62:11. Think back as well to earlier passages where "the day" was vividly described (for example, Isa. 13:9–13). *Note: the nation of Edom (literally "red"), with its capital city Bozrah (literally "vintage"), was made up of Esau's descendants. Edom fought against God's people for centuries, and often in Scripture comes to represent those who will receive God's final judgment (recall Isa. 34).*

2. Consider how Isaiah 63:1–6 stretches our understanding of *salvation*.

   a. Summarize the dramatic situation of these verses.

    b.   In Isaiah 63:1, what is communicated about this figure, and how?

    c.   What strong and repeated words stand out in this passage?

    d.   What does this figure show us about God, and why is it often hard for us to take this in?

3. Look at the context of this passage. What is the effect of finding Isaiah 63:1–6 following and preceding the verses it follows and precedes?

4. The scriptural context of this passage reaches all the way to the end of the Bible. Read and meditate on Revelation 14:14–20 and 19:11–16. Write down your observations.

5. How comprehensively do we believe in this splendid, righteous Savior who came, who suffered and died for us, who rose from the dead, who reigns in heaven, and who will come again in all his glory? How should such a belief affect the way we serve him even now, as we live in this interval of favor between the first and second lines of Isaiah 61:2?

DAY FIVE—CONCLUSIONS

1. What a mercy that we serve a "speaking" God who reveals himself and his salvation to us supremely in his glorious Son. How amazing that he reveals even his plans for all eternity—and that those plans include all his creation. Look back through the chapters we have studied, asking what God is revealing concerning himself, his attributes, and his way of dealing with human beings. Write down several aspects of God that stand out to you, and then write your personal response—which could be in the form of a prayer, or questions, or simply a few sentences responding to the Lord God who speaks his salvation to us in his Word.

2. Look once more through the section and choose a verse or a short passage to write out and commit to memory.

Be ready to share with your group the ways in which you find the verse (or verses) challenging, helpful, beautiful, etc.

Notes for Lesson 22

Lesson 23 (Isaiah 63:7–65:16)

THE LORD READY TO BE SOUGHT AND FOUND

DAY ONE—REMEMBERING THE LORD (ISAIAH 63:7–19)

1. Right after the intense focus on his wrath and judgment, what *attributes* and *actions* of the Lord does Isaiah recount in Isaiah 63:7–9? Is there one line here that for you gets most closely to the heart of God's steadfast love? Explain. *Note this "steadfast love" (Hebrew "hesed") enclosing verse 7—a word used throughout the Old Testament to express God's merciful covenant love for his people.*

2. Isaiah 63:10–14 recounts God's steadfast love by recalling a specific historical context.

    a.   How does verse 10 describe the problem? How does each second line reveal God more deeply?

    b.   Isaiah 63:11–14 recalls the days of Moses—and evokes what sorts of realizations and questions?

    c.   Isaiah richly presents God in three persons, as we have consistently seen. What do we see of God in Isaiah's three references to the Holy Spirit in this passage?

d. How would you express the main point of this little passage?

3. This recounting leads to prayer—the prayer of a people who have wandered from God and who want to return. It might be the prayer of a people in exile. It is the prayer of sinners, a prayer that must begin by looking up to a holy God. In Isaiah 63:15–17, what truths are acknowledged about God and about the speaker's (and then the speakers') relationship with God?

4. On the basis of such acknowledgements, what is appropriate about the words to God in Isaiah 63:17–19?

DAY TWO—DEEP INTO PRAYER (ISAIAH 64:1–12)

1. The prayer continues with an amazing plea. Read Isaiah 64:1–3 (as well as Ex. 19:10–20). For what are these people longing? What pictures and repeated words stand out?

2. Consider and comment on the way Isaiah 64:4–5 exhibits both *faith* and *questioning*. Even from this rather dark place, what verbs express what these people know they must do?

3. How do the words and images in Isaiah 64:6–7 portray the gravity of sin? *Note: An "unclean" person, according to Old Testament law, was one unfit to be in the presence of God or his people (Lev. 13:45–46). A "polluted garment" means literally "a garment of menstruation" (Lev. 15:19).*

4. "But now," in Isaiah 64:8–9, begins the leading of people out of darkness. What is the plea, the tone of the plea, and the basis of the plea?

5. What are the focus and tone of Isaiah 64:10–12? (Recall Isa. 62:1.)

6. Look back through Isaiah 64:1–12. In what ways does this prayer challenge and instruct you?

DAY THREE—GOD ANSWERS
CLEARLY (ISAIAH 65:1–10)

1. The longing of the prayer we have just read is bearable
   because we have seen the answer to that longing, in the
   Lord himself and in his revealed plan of redemption.
   Read Isaiah 65:1–2 along with Romans 10:11–21.
   What aspects of God and of his salvation stand out
   in these verses?

2. Ponder the charges against God's people in Isaiah 65:2–7.

   a. What do you find at the heart of these evils? What
      words stand out?

b. How would you characterize God's response to these evils? What do we learn here?

3. In the midst of such disobedience, hope has glimmered from the start (see Isa. 1:9). Read Isaiah 65:8 (and recall 5:1–4). What hope shines in this picture? *Note: Read on in the Romans passage we just consulted, to find this hope confirmed (Rom. 11:1–8).*

4. How do these promises grow, in Isaiah 65:9–10? What phrases describe the people who will enjoy the fulfillment of these promises? *Note: the desolation and judgment of Sharon (Isa. 33:9) and Achor (Josh. 7:24–26) will be transformed.*

DAY FOUR—TWO DIFFERENT ETERNAL REWARDS (ISAIAH 65:11–16)

1. After a vision of such blessing, what contrasts appear in Isaiah 65:11–12? What characteristics of these people stand out, in contrast with those to whom we have listened in Isaiah 64? *Note: Fortune and Destiny were names of pagan false gods.*

2. What do you observe in the list of contrasting rewards in Isaiah 65:13–15? Why might these verses be hard to digest? Why are they important to read?

3. What might be this other name God calls his servants (Isa. 65:15–16)? Before answering, recall Isaiah 62:2–4, 12.

4. In Isaiah 65:16, what is the main point in these words about oaths and blessings?

5. We shall look into these promised blessings in the final lesson. With the last lines of Isaiah 65:16, we prepare to turn our focus from "former troubles" of sorrow and sin to the "new heavens" and "new earth." To prepare for the final lesson, read through to the book's end.

DAY FIVE—CONCLUSIONS

1. How beautiful to find such a personal, penitent, powerful prayer here in Isaiah's closing chapters. How amazing to see again the personal response of God to his people—a people who come ultimately from every nation, and only through the work of King Jesus, the Suffering Servant, the final Conqueror and Judge. Look through the chapters we have studied, focusing on the Lord God of our salvation. What do we learn of him, his attributes, and his way of

dealing with human beings? Write down several aspects of God that stand out to you, and then write your personal response—which could be in the form of a prayer, or questions, or simply a few sentences responding to this Lord God who indeed hears our humble, heartfelt prayers.

2. Look once more through the lesson and choose a verse or a short passage to write out and commit to memory. Be ready to share with your group the ways in which you find the verse (or verses) challenging, helpful, beautiful, etc.

Notes for Lesson 23

Lesson 24
(Isaiah 65:17–66:24)

THE LORD SAVES AND JUDGES

In finishing this lesson, we will have read the entire book of Isaiah. To the end, his vision combines a vivid, close-up look at sin with a many-layered, far-reaching look at God's plan for redeeming a people out of sin and into his presence in that new Jerusalem. His vision stretches far in these final chapters—all the way into eternity.

DAY ONE—THE NEW HEAVENS AND NEW EARTH (ISAIAH 65:17–25)

1. Isaiah 65:17, beginning with "For," opens an even fuller explanation of the blessings just promised to the Lord's faithful servants. Along with this verse, recall Genesis 1:1 and Genesis 3. Jot down your comments and observations.

2. Before the re-creation at the end of human history, what will happen to the original creation? What can we observe in Peter's description, in 2 Peter 3:1–13?

3. The "former things" will not be remembered, or brought to mind, we're told. This is not a memory lapse but rather a new focus. What things can we observe about this new focus, in Isaiah 65:18?

4. Two other passages ask to be read along with this section. For the remainder of this day's study, first read carefully Isaiah 65:17–25. Second, read one more time Isaiah 11:1–10. Then turn to the end of the story and reread (one more time!) Revelation 21. As you

read, jot down common themes and words—all of which will be helpful as we continue.

DAY TWO—A NEW JERUSALEM
(ISAIAH 65:17–25 . . . AGAIN!)

Isaiah lets us peer into the New Jerusalem—the one God will establish finally and perfectly in his new creation at the end of human history. From Isaiah's first chapter, we have watched Jerusalem as the central picture of God's gathered people, with its temple on Mount Zion showing the beauty of true worship in God's presence. We have seen the sinful corruption that assailed this city. We have glimpsed God's plan for this city to be purified and renewed, and to draw people from all the nations, through the saving work of the Messiah. In these concluding chapters, the overarching theme we noted in Lesson One is complete: God will indeed save his people forever in the New Jerusalem.

1. Jerusalem has never been just a literal city, in Isaiah. What do the parallel lines in Isaiah 65:18cd, 19ab tell us about

its true substance? Examine God's expressions toward this city in these lines. What do you learn, and how do you respond?

2. Promises of blessing in this city come next. In Isaiah 65:19–20, what kind of hope and what kind of existence do these phrases promise to the people of God? *Note: These verses are difficult, as they mention death and sinners, but there is no death and no sin (and no babies born) in the new heavens and new earth. (Review Rev. 20:14–21:27.) Some readers conclude that this passage presents the thousand-year reign of Christ described in Revelation 20:4–6 (<u>before</u> the final new heavens and new earth). However, whatever one's view of the millennium, this Isaiah passage corresponds to Revelation 21, not Revelation 20. Isaiah 65:17–25 begins with the main idea of the new heavens and new earth, as does Revelation 21, and both describe the heavenly hope of rejoicing eternally (with no more weeping) in God's presence with God's people in the New Jerusalem. Might verses 20–25 change time focus, moving back to a millennial state which leads into the final new heavens and new earth? Indeed, Isaiah is consistently concerned more with content than chronology. However, he does make passages clearly flow, and this one seems to flow in unity from verse 17 to verse 25, with the*

New Jerusalem explicitly described from verse 18 on. How, then, might one reconcile Isaiah's insertions of death and sin into his vision of the new heavens and new earth? One widely accepted possibility is to understand that Isaiah's language here (as elsewhere) is freely poetic, expressing eternal realities by using exaggerated pictures from the world we know. In this new order, for example, a hundred years would feel like time had hardly moved. We must keep studying such rich but complicated passages, especially within the whole counsel of Scripture. But we must not forget to glean the hope they hold.

3. How does Isaiah 65:21–23 show the inhabitants of this city to have overcome the effects of the curse of sin? What kinds of sorrows are gone, and what kinds of joys are present?

4. What does Isaiah 65:24 show about the relationship of God with his people in this city? What previous verses might this verse bring to mind?

5. Finally, in this picture of God's holy mountain (Mount Zion, Jerusalem), in what ways has all creation been set right, according to the lines of Isaiah 65:25? What do we see here concerning the nature of God's redemption?

DAY THREE—TREMBLE AT HIS WORD (ISAIAH 66:1–11)

The final chapter of Isaiah completes the vision that includes not only the blessings of New Jerusalem but the punishment of those who have rebelled. Until we reach that city, the "former things" must be remembered, so that salvation can be proclaimed to all nations. The chapter begins with the Lord in heaven, the vantage point where all time and place come into focus.

1. The Lord is not condemning the building or rebuilding of the temple, in Isaiah 66:1–2. What is the point here? What is the warning and the urging?

2. Isaiah 66:3–4 shows the worthless sacrifices of those who miss the starting point of this chapter. Examine the list of sacrifices according to Old Testament law, paired with sacrifices contrary to Old Testament law. One is as good as the other, without *what*? How does the Lord articulate the nature of their punishment, and the reasons for it? (Recall Isa. 65:12.)

3. Examine the references to God *speaking*, God's *word*, etc., in Isaiah 66:1–5b. How is his *word* the central point here—and how does this emphasis appropriately conclude the whole book?

4. What is the context, and what is the encouragement for those who tremble at God's word, in Isaiah 66:5? What dramatic hint in verse 6 encourages these faithful ones to persevere?

5. The encouragement for the faithful continues—in fact, it overflows! Read Isaiah 66:7–11.

   a. How is Jerusalem pictured here, and what does this picture communicate?

   b. How does this picture bring resolution to similar pictures we have seen?

   c. How might details and aspects of this picture encourage you even today?

Day Four—Final Glory and Judgment (Isaiah 66:12–24)

1. We were not finished with that image of "Mother Jerusalem"! In Isaiah 66:12–14, in what ways does the Lord emerge as the one behind that image? What aspects of the Lord and his promises are emphasized here? Muse on these rich words and take them in, as personally from the Lord.

2. The last line of verse 14 leads to the next wave of contrast—again turning to God's judgment on those who are not his servants. In Isaiah 66:15–16, how do we glimpse the answer to Isaiah 64:1–2, for those who have rejected him? What is verse 17's focus in portraying this final judgment?

3. Isaiah 66:18–21 makes another turn toward the prospect of God's multiplying his people, gathering them from all the nations, before that final judgment comes.

   a. What repeated word tells us what God wants the nations to see? What will be the "sign" of this (v. 19)? (See Isa. 7:14; 11:10; John 1:14.)

   b. These "survivors" (v. 19) are probably the believers who persevere—true offspring of the Lord. In Isaiah 66:19–20, what do we see these survivors doing, and how might their activity relate to Matthew 24:3–14 and 28:19–20? *Note: The locations named are real places, in all directions throughout Isaiah's known world—a picture of the whole world.*

   c.   The idea of non-Jews serving as priests would have shocked Old Testament Jews. What is the glorious truth of the picture in Isaiah 66:21? (See Ex. 19:5–6; Isa. 61:6; 1 Peter 2:9–10.)

4. Isaiah 66:22–23 offers Isaiah's final, beautiful word from God on the certainty of the promises he has set forth. How is this picture of true, eternal worship a fitting one with which to end? (Recall where we began, in Isa. 1:12–14.)

5. Isaiah does not end without one more dark turn, in Isaiah 66:24. He paints a picture (probably using the garbage dump outside Jerusalem as his source) of the inhabitants of the new heavens and new earth going out to look

on the eternal punishment of those who have rebelled against the Lord God. This is a picture of the reality of hell. (See Mark 9:47–48.) In light of Isaiah's whole prophecy, how do such words appropriately conclude this book?

Day Five—Conclusions

1. Think, on this final day, of where we have come in Isaiah. Look back through Isaiah 1 as well as these final chapters we have studied, in order to see again the whole vision Isaiah has developed so beautifully— of the Holy One of Israel who mercifully redeems a sinful people, according to his word and through his own righteousness and justice found in his Son. Truly Isaiah tells the story of his own name: "The Lord saves." This saving is of a people . . . the people of the true Jerusalem . . . the Jerusalem that will finally spread out to embrace the whole earth. What a large vision of the gospel story God granted to this prophet. As you review these chapters, looking up to the Lord on

his throne, what do you see? What do you hear that especially penetrates your heart? Write your response.

2. One more final review—of the figure that looms centrally in Isaiah's vision, the one by whom God will accomplish this salvation. Simply reread and rejoice in these passages from each of the three main sections of the book, in order to see again this King/Servant/Anointed Conqueror who, as we have seen, is our Lord and Savior Jesus Christ: Isaiah 9:2–7; 52:13–53:12; 61:1–7.

3. Look once more through these last chapters and choose a verse or a short passage to write out and commit to memory. Be ready to share with your group the ways in which you find the verse (or verses) challenging, helpful, beautiful, etc. Look back through all the "Day Five" verses

you have chosen: how will it affect you to keep on hiding these verses in your heart?

Notes for Lesson 24

Notes for Leaders

What a privilege it is to lead a group in studying the Word of God! Following are six principles offered to help guide you as you lead.

1. The Primacy of the Biblical Text

If you forget all the other principles, I encourage you to hold on to this one! The Bible is God speaking to us, through his inspired Word—living and active and sharper than a two-edged sword. As leaders, we aim to point people as effectively as possible into this Word. We can trust the Bible to do all that God intends in the lives of those studying with us.

This means that the job of a leader is to direct the conversation of a group constantly back into the text. If you "get stuck," usually the best thing to say is: "Let's go back to the text and read it again." The questions in this study aim to lead people into the text, rather than into a swirl of personal opinions about the topics of the text; therefore, depending on the questions should help. Personal opinions and experiences will often enrich your group's interactions; however, many Bible studies these days have moved almost exclusively into the realm of "What does this mean to me?" rather than first trying to get straight on "What does this mean?"

We'll never understand the text perfectly, but we can stand on one of the great principles of the Reformation: the *perspicuity* of Scripture. This simply means *understandability*. God made us word-creatures, in his image, and he gave us a Word that he wants us to understand more and more, with careful reading and study, and shared counsel and prayer.

The primacy of the text implies less of a dependence on commentaries and answer guides than often has been the case. I do not offer answers to the questions, because the answers are in the biblical text, and we desperately need to learn how to dig in and find them. When individuals articulate what they find for themselves (leaders included!), they have learned more, with each of their answers, about studying God's Word. These competencies are then transferable and applicable in every other study of the Bible. Without a set of answers, a leader will not be an "answer person," but rather a fellow searcher of the Scriptures.

Helps *are* helpful in the right place! It is good to keep at hand a Bible dictionary of some kind. The lessons themselves actually offer context and help with the questions as they are asked. A few commentaries are listed in the "Notes on Translations and Study Helps," and these can give further guidance after one has spent good time with the text itself. I place great importance as well on the help of leaders and teachers in one's church, which leads us into the second principle.

2. The Context of the Church

As Christians, we have a new identity: we are part of the body of Christ. According to the New Testament, that body is clearly meant to live and work in local bodies, local churches. The ideal context for Bible study is within a church body—one that is reaching out in all directions to the people around it. (Bible studies can be the best places for evangelism!) I realize that these studies will be used in all kinds of ways and places; but whatever the context, I would hope that the group leaders have a layer of solid church leaders around them, people to whom they can go with questions and concerns as they study the Scriptures. When a leader doesn't know the answer to a question that arises, it's really OK to say, "I don't know. But I'll be happy to try to find out." Then that leader can go to pastors and teachers, as well as to commentaries, to learn more.

The church context has many ramifications for Bible study. For example, when a visitor attends a study and comes to know the Lord, the visitor—and his or her family—can be plugged into the context of the church. For another example, what happens in a Bible study often can be integrated with other courses of study within the church, and even with the preaching, so that the whole body learns and grows together. This depends, of course, on the connection of those leading the study with those leading the church—a connection that I have found to be most fruitful and encouraging.

3. THE IMPORTANCE OF PLANNING AND THINKING AHEAD

How many of us have experienced the rush to get to Bible study on time . . . or have jumped in without thinking through what will happen during the precious minutes of group interaction . . . or have felt out of control as we've made our way through a quarter of the questions and used up three-quarters of the time! It is crucial, after having worked through the lesson yourself, to think it through from the perspective of leading the discussion. How will you open the session, giving perhaps a nutshell statement of the main theme and the central goals for the day? (Each lesson offers a brief introduction that will help with the opening.) Which questions do you not want to miss discussing, and which ones could you quickly summarize or even skip? How much time would you like to allot for the different sections of the study?

If you're leading a group by yourself, you will need to prepare extra carefully—and that can be done! If you're part of a larger study, perhaps with multiple small groups, it's helpful for the various group leaders to meet together and to help each other with the planning. Often, a group of leaders meets early on the morning of a study, in order to help the others with the fruit of their study, plan the group time, and pray—which leads into the fourth principle.

4. THE CRUCIAL ROLE OF PRAYER

If these words we're studying are truly the inspired Word of God, then how much we need to ask for his Spirit's help and guidance as we study his revelation! This is a prayer found often in Scripture itself, and a prayer God evidently loves to answer: that he would give us understanding of his truth, according to his Word. I encourage you as a leader to pray before and as you work through the lesson, to encourage those in your group to do the same, to model this kind of prayer as you lead the group time, to pray for your group members by name throughout the week, and to ask one or two "prayer warriors" in your life to pray for you as you lead.

5. THE SENSITIVE ART OF LEADING

Whole manuals, of course, have been written on this subject! Actually, the four principles preceding this one may be most fundamental in cultivating your group leadership ability. Again, I encourage you to consider yourself not as a person with all the right answers, but rather as one who studies along with the people in your group—and who then facilitates the group members' discussion of all they have discovered in the Scriptures.

There is always a tension between pouring out the wisdom of all your own preparation and knowledge, on the one hand,

and encouraging those in your group to relish and share all they have learned, on the other. I advise leaders to lean more heavily toward the latter, reserving the former to steer gently and wisely through a well-planned group discussion. What we're trying to accomplish is not to cement our own roles as leaders, but to participate in God's work of raising up mature Christians who know how to study and understand the Word—and who will themselves become equipped to lead.

With specific issues in group leading—such as encouraging everybody to talk, or handling one who talks too much—I encourage you to seek the counsel of one with experience in leading groups. There is no better help than the mentoring and prayerful support of a wise person who has been there! That's even better than the best "how-to" manual. If you have a number of group leaders, perhaps you will invite an experienced group leader to come and conduct a practical session on how to lead.

Remember: the default move is, "Back to the text!"

6. THE POWER OF THE SCRIPTURES TO DELIGHT

Finally, in the midst of it all, let us not forget to delight together in the Scriptures! We should be serious but not joyless! In fact, we as leaders should model for our groups a growing and satisfying delight in the Word of God—as we notice its beauty, stop to linger over a lovely word or phrase, enjoy the poetry, appreciate the shape of a passage from beginning to end, laugh at a touch of irony or an image that hits home, wonder over a truth that pierces the soul.

May we share and spread the response of Jeremiah, who said:

> Your words were found, and I ate them,
> and your words became to me a joy
> and the delight of my heart. (Jer. 15:16)

OUTLINE OF ISAIAH

The Preface (Chapters 1–5)

The Call (Chapter 6)

The Main Sections of the Book:

CHAPTERS	TIME REFERENCED	WHO ACTS?
I. 7–39	*Pre-Exile* *(Assyrian domination)*	*The King*
II. 40–55	*Exile* *(Babylonian domination)*	*The Servant*
III. 56–66	*Post-Exile* *(Persian domination)*	*The Anointed* *Conqueror*

Subsections to keep in mind:

Ia. Chapters 7–12: Words of judgment and hope in relation to King Ahaz

Ib. Chapters 13–23: Oracles addressed to the nations

Ic. Chapters 24–27: A far view to the end: Two Cities

Id. Chapters 28–35: Six woes—all about trusting the one true God

Ie. Chapters 36–39: King Hezekiah's story, in a *bridge section*—looking back to Assyria in chapters 36–37, and ahead to Babylon in chapters 38–39

The Servant Songs embedded in Section II:

IIa. The first Servant Song (Isa. 42:1–9)

IIb. The second Servant Song (Isa. 49:1–6)

IIc. The third Servant Song (Isa. 50:4–11)

IId. The fourth Servant Song (Isa. 52:13–53:12)

TIMELINES AND MAP OF ISAIAH'S WORLD

- General Timeline
- Detailed Timeline
- Map of Isaiah's World

General Timeline

Timelines reflect best approximations of commentators referenced in the Notes.

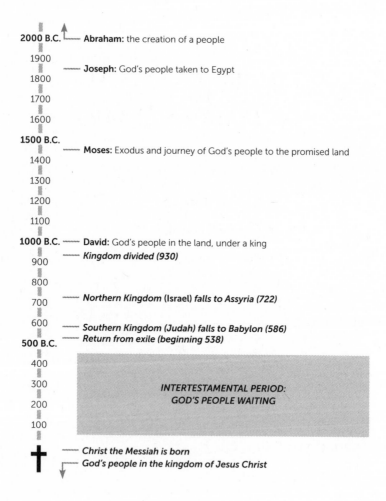

2000 B.C. —— **Abraham:** the creation of a people

1900

—— **Joseph:** God's people taken to Egypt

1800

1700

1600

1500 B.C.

—— **Moses:** Exodus and journey of God's people to the promised land

1400

1300

1200

1100

1000 B.C. —— **David:** God's people in the land, under a king

900 —— *Kingdom divided (930)*

800

700 —— *Northern Kingdom (Israel) falls to Assyria (722)*

600 —— *Southern Kingdom (Judah) falls to Babylon (586)*

500 B.C. —— *Return from exile (beginning 538)*

400

300   *INTERTESTAMENTAL PERIOD:*

200   *GOD'S PEOPLE WAITING*

100

—— *Christ the Messiah is born*

—— *God's people in the kingdom of Jesus Christ*

Detailed Timeline
Events referenced in Isaiah

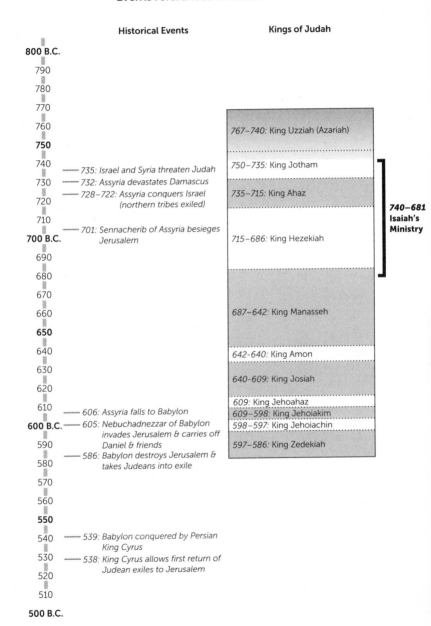

Historical Events

Kings of Judah

800 B.C.
790
780
770
760
750
740
730
720
710
700 B.C.
690
680
670
660
650
640
630
620
610
600 B.C.
590
580
570
560
550
540
530
520
510
500 B.C.

767–740: King Uzziah (Azariah)

750–735: King Jotham

735: Israel and Syria threaten Judah
732: Assyria devastates Damascus
728–722: Assyria conquers Israel
(northern tribes exiled)

735–715: King Ahaz

701: Sennacherib of Assyria besieges
Jerusalem

715–686: King Hezekiah

740–681
Isaiah's
Ministry

687–642: King Manasseh

642-640: King Amon

640-609: King Josiah

609: King Jehoahaz
606: Assyria falls to Babylon
609–598: King Jehoiakim
605: Nebuchadnezzar of Babylon
598–597: King Jehoiachin
invades Jerusalem & carries off
Daniel & friends
597–586: King Zedekiah
586: Babylon destroys Jerusalem &
takes Judeans into exile

539: Babylon conquered by Persian
King Cyrus
538: King Cyrus allows first return of
Judean exiles to Jerusalem

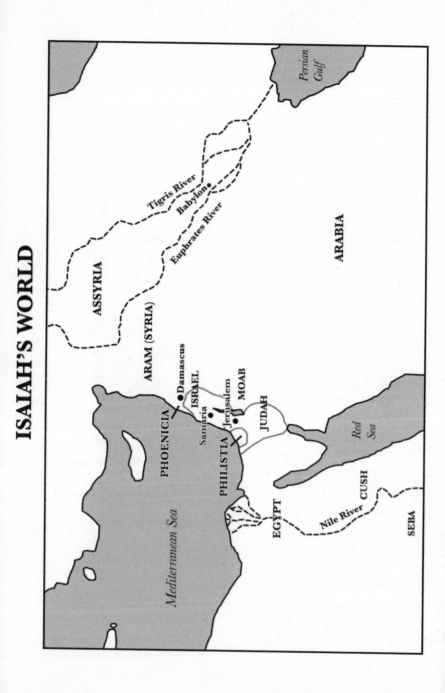

SUGGESTED
MEMORY PASSAGES

It shall come to pass in the latter days
    that the mountain of the house of the LORD
shall be established as the highest of the mountains,
    and shall be lifted up above the hills;
and all the nations shall flow to it,
    and many peoples shall come, and say:
"Come, let us go up to the mountain of the LORD,
    to the house of the God of Jacob,
that he may teach us his ways
    and that we may walk in his paths."
For out of Zion shall go the law,
    and the word of the LORD from Jerusalem.
He shall judge between the nations,
    and shall decide disputes for many peoples;
and they shall beat their swords into plowshares,
    and their spears into pruning hooks;
nation shall not lift up sword against nation,
    neither shall they learn war anymore.
O house of Jacob,
    come, let us walk
    in the light of the LORD. (Isa. 2:2–5)

In that day this song will be sung in the land of Judah:

"We have a strong city;
    he sets up salvation
    as walls and bulwarks.
Open the gates,
    that the righteous nation that keeps faith may enter
        in.
You keep him in perfect peace
    whose mind is stayed on you,
    because he trusts in you.
Trust in the LORD forever,
    for the LORD GOD is an everlasting rock."
        (Isa. 26:1–4)

Behold, my servant shall act wisely;
    he shall be high and lifted up,
    and shall be exalted.
As many were astonished at you—
    his appearance was so marred, beyond human
        semblance,
    and his form beyond that of the children of
        mankind—
so shall he sprinkle many nations;
    kings shall shut their mouths because of him;
for that which has not been told them they see,
    and that which they have not heard they
        understand.
Who has believed what they heard from us?
    And to whom has the arm of the LORD been
        revealed?
For he grew up before him like a young plant,
    and like a root out of dry ground;

he had no form or majesty that we should look at him,
    and no beauty that we should desire him.
He was despised and rejected by men;
    a man of sorrows and acquainted with grief;
and as one from whom men hide their faces
    he was despised, and we esteemed him not.
Surely he has borne our griefs
    and carried our sorrows;
yet we esteemed him stricken,
    smitten by God, and afflicted.
But he was wounded for our transgressions;
    he was crushed for our iniquities;
upon him was the chastisement that brought us peace,
    and with his stripes we are healed.
All we like sheep have gone astray;
    we have turned everyone to his own way;
and the LORD has laid on him
    the iniquity of us all. (Isa. 52:13–53:6)

The Spirit of the Lord GOD is upon me,
    because the LORD has anointed me
to bring good news to the poor;
    he has sent me to bind up the brokenhearted,
to proclaim liberty to the captives,
    and the opening of the prison to those who are
        bound;
to proclaim the year of the LORD's favor,
    and the day of vengeance of our God;
    to comfort all who mourn;
to grant to those who mourn in Zion—
    to give them a beautiful headdress instead of ashes,
the oil of gladness instead of mourning,
    the garment of praise instead of a faint spirit;

that they may be called oaks of righteousness,
    the planting of the LORD, that he may be glorified.
They shall build up the ancient ruins;
    they shall raise up the former devastations;
they shall repair the ruined cities,
    the devastations of many generations. (Isa. 61:1–4)

NOTES ON TRANSLATIONS
AND STUDY HELPS

This study can be done with any reliable translation of the Bible, although I do recommend the English Standard Version for its essentially literal but beautifully readable translation of the original languages. In preparing this study, I have used and quoted from the English Standard Version, published by Crossway Bibles in Wheaton, Illinois.

These lessons may be completed with only the Bible open in front of you. The point is to grapple with the text, not with what others have said about the text. The goal is to know, increasingly, the joy and reward of digging into the Scriptures, God's breathed-out words which not only are able to make us wise for salvation through faith in Christ Jesus, but also are profitable for teaching, reproof, correction, and training in righteousness, that each of us may be competent, equipped for every good work (2 Tim. 3:15–17). To help you dig in, basic and helpful contexts and comments are given throughout the lessons. I have used and learned from the following books in my own study and preparation; you may find sources such as these helpful at some point.

General Handbooks:

The Crossway Comprehensive Concordance of the Holy Bible: English Standard Version. Compiled by William D. Mounce. Wheaton: Crossway Books, 2002. (Other concordances are available, from various publishers and for other translations.)

The Illustrated Bible Dictionary. 4 vols. Wheaton: Tyndale House Publishers, 1980. (The *Zondervan Pictorial Encyclopedia of the Bible* is similarly helpful.)

Ryken, Leland, James Wilhoit, and Tremper Longman III, eds. *Dictionary of Biblical Imagery.* Downers Grove, IL: InterVarsity Press, 1998.

Ryken, Leland, Philip Ryken, and James Wilhoit. *Ryken's Bible Handbook.* Wheaton: Tyndale House Publishers, 2005.

Vine's Complete Expository Dictionary of Old and New Testament Words. Nashville: Thomas Nelson, 1984.

Commentaries and Helps:

Calvin, John. *Isaiah.* Crossway Classic Commentary Series. Wheaton: Crossway Books, 2000.

Jackman, David. *Teaching Isaiah: Unlocking Isaiah for the Bible Teacher.* Ross-shire, Scotland: Christian Focus Publications Ltd., with Proclamation Trust Media, 2010.

Kidner, Derek. "Isaiah." *New Bible Commentary.* Edited by D. Guthrie and J. A. Motyer. Leicester, England: InterVarsity Press, 1970. 588–625.

Motyer, J. Alec. *Isaiah: An Introduction and Commentary.* Tyndale Old Testament Commentary Series. Downers Grove, IL: InterVarsity Press, 1999.

Ortlund, Raymond C. Jr. *Isaiah: God Saves Sinners.* Preaching the Word Series. Wheaton: Crossway Books, 2005.

Study Bible:

ESV Study Bible. English Standard Version. Wheaton: Crossway Bibles, 2008.

Kathleen Nielson (MA, PhD in literature, Vanderbilt University) has taught in the English departments at Vanderbilt University, Bethel College (Minnesota), and Wheaton College. She is the author of numerous Bible studies, the book *Bible Study: Following the Ways of the Word*, and various articles and poems. Kathleen has directed and taught women's Bible studies at several churches and speaks extensively at conferences and retreats. She serves as advisor and editor for The Gospel Coalition and was its director of women's initiatives from 2010–2017. She is also on the board of directors of The Charles Simeon Trust.

Kathleen and her husband Niel have three sons, two beautiful daughters-in-law, and a growing number of grandchildren!